LOST WITHOUT MY DAUGHTER

LOST WITHOUT MY DAUGHTER

BY

SAYED MAHMOODY

This edition published in 2013 by:

Thistle Publishing
36 Great Smith Street
London
SW1P 3BU

ISBN-13: 978-1-909869-79-0

PROLOGUE
JANUARY 14, 1986

The ambulance screamed up the street towards our apartment. I sighed with resignation; my breath frosted in the evening air.

It had been a cold winter; snow had fallen thick and heavy and was knee-deep in our yard. Mahtob and I had made a snowman: a carrot for the nose, walnuts for the eyes.

Mahtob, who was five-years-old, took her purple scarf. "He'll get cold without it!" she exclaimed and so I, laughing and proud of my daughter's consideration, wrapped it tightly round his neck. There had been no more snowfall since that day but the long winter meant that our snowman was still there, shrinking but holding on.

It was rare to see the city blanketed in white. Tehran sits high on a bone-dry plateau; it almost never rains but it is watered by the snow-melt from the enormous Elburz and Zagros mountains that encircle the city; jagged, dizzying peaks which rise to a breathless 19,000 feet; divided only by sheer gorges sliced by icy water.

The ambulance slid to a stop; the driver yelled that victims from a chemical weapons attack needed my attention urgently. Five young men had already died in our hospital that week, the result of mustard-gas bombs dropped during fighting on the western bank of the Shatt al-Arab, the southern river border between Iran and Iraq. At least, as an anaesthetist I was able to make their deaths relatively painless.

"I've got to go," I shouted to Betty while slushing my way to the vehicle, "I'll call you as soon as I know how bad it is." We had a dinner appointment with our neighbours and Betty didn't want to miss it.

"Okay Moody," she called back, "We'll start without you!"

I blew Mahtob a kiss, which she returned, "Goodbye Mahtob, take care of our snowman!"

"I will, Daddy," she replied in Farsi, waving her gloved hand frantically. The wailing ambulance jolted as it span its wheels and whisked me away out of our exclusive district, past the old, deserted palace of the long-gone Shah which sat below the snow-covered mountains, and through the chaotic traffic to the emergency room of Shohadye Tajrish Hospital.

CHAPTER ONE
HOLLYWOOD ENDING

The day of the snowman was the last time I ever spent any time with my daughter. For a few weeks after Betty and Mahtob disappeared I wondered whether I would ever see them again - until a friend arrived phoned to tell me that he had just seen Betty on national US Television.

I thought my heart was going to burst straight through my ribcage. I watched, first in disbelief and then through tears as Betty told the world that I had kidnapped her and Mahtob, forced them to stay in Iran and had beaten them. She then said they had escaped over the Zagros Mountains to the United States.

I was astounded beyond belief; *I* had beaten *Betty*? Beaten my beloved Mahtob? They'd escaped over the *Zagros Mountains*? Surely nobody could travel over the Zagros Mountains in January? They stretch as far as the Alps and are as broad as Switzerland. Snow and ice make them impassable.

Betty also announced she was writing a book about her 'terrible ordeal'.

I collapsed back into my chair and sat for – well, I don't know how long – trying to absorb what I'd just learned.

At least I now knew they were in the US. I called Betty's parents.

Betty's sister Carolyn answered. "You forced Betty and Mahtob to stay in Iran," she yelled "You treated them like shit, Moody. Don't even think about coming over here. The day Betty got back she filed complaints against you. The police have told the State to refuse you entry. You gotta forget about Betty and Mahtob forever.'

The line went dead.

I looked at the floor, my head in my hands. I was a fool. How could I have been so blind? Why did I try for so long to keep us together? Mahtob. Yes, it was because of Mahtob. We had both stuck it out for her sake.

I had once mocked Betty's intelligence but now it was clear she had outsmarted me by some way. She was in the US with Mahtob, and with the country 100% behind her story, while I, the evil monster, was trapped in Iran.

Life goes on and, to cope, I worked ever harder at the hospital. Whenever an extra pair of hands was needed I stepped forward and I lingered at the end of my shifts. I loved my work; but although I won the admiration of my colleagues, I made enemies of the Ministry of Health.

A member of the hospital's Islamic Society had told me to grow a beard and to stop wearing Western suits. I ignored him. A few days later I received a letter. The language was typical of the revolution.

'A man named Sayed Bozorg Mahmoody is not a real doctor,' it said. 'He is a quack, working illegally. As of this date he is not allowed to work as a physician.'

My stubbornness and notoriety (my predicament made me famous in Iran) had cost me my license. Luckily, thanks to my family background I was able to persuade some influential people to intercede so that I could practice medicine again. The Ministry agreed to take me back after I had done some re-training and soon I had returned – still wearing a suit and still clean-shaven.

Months passed. One afternoon, Farik[1], a fellow doctor and wily friend popped his head through my door. Tall and thin with mischievous eyes, Farik was an inveterate gossip and always first with any news; he had impeccable sources from various other gossips throughout Tehran. He'd taken great interest in my story and had followed me incessantly around the hospital trying to squeeze juicy details from me. Oddly enough, as much as I tried to resist him at first, Farik was very likeable and we eventually became firm friends. He held a fearless and unhealthy disregard for the Pasdaran[2] and once he was your friend he was totally loyal.

"Brace yourself," Farik told me and handed me a book.

I stared at the cover: '*Not Without My Daughter by Betty Mahmoody.*'

---

1 In the interests of his safety, I've changed Farik's name.
2 Secret Police

Farik left me to it. I locked the door and sank into my chair. The first thing that struck me about the book was the size - it was so thick. Was there really that much to our story?

It took me a while to bring myself to read it. And when I did, it nearly killed me. When I finally finished it and put it down on the coffee table I felt physically sick.

In the book Betty described the joy with which she packed to go home at the end of what she described as our 'two-week holiday' in Iran and my strange behaviour, the deep depression she saw in my face, and how my 'eyes grew dim and void, like those of so many other Iranians'. She also wrote that she loathed my homeland, my family and me.

Betty was not treated as an outcast; my sister Ameh did not grow less cordial. Neither did Ameh complain about our 'wasteful American habit' of showering every day. My sister did not bathe just once a week; she did not wear the same filthy clothes day after day, despite the searing heat. She did not - and neither did any member of my family – 'stink'.

Our daughter was not 'covered in mosquito bites', nor did she have '23 bites on her face alone.' A stew did not 'bubble incessantly on the stove for the convenience of anyone who was hungry'. People did not 'take sips from it and allow the residue from their mouths to drip back into the pot or dribble onto the floor.' The floors were not 'honeycombed with trails of sugar left by careless tea drinkers'. A cockroach has never appeared in my sister's house - if it did it would not survive very long. Food did not have a 'rancid taste that appeals to the Iranian palate'.

Tehran was not as grim as Betty said it was, people smiled and laughed and enjoyed life, despite the war with Iraq. Their lives were not 'shabby', people did not 'drink from the gutters' of Tehran, nor did they urinate in them.

Betty did not wear a veil, much less one 'covered in dried spittle'. No one in my family ever wiped their nose on a veil, let alone carried on wearing it.

I could not understand why, in her book Betty said that she had not told her mother and father that she was going to Iran with me. She explained that they would worry. But it seems incredible to me not to mention such a trip to one's parents. And besides, they did know. They knew everything.

We did not sacrifice a sheep on Betty's arrival and cover the floor with blood. The kitchen was clean, its appliances were not rusty, the sink was not piled with dirty dishes and food was not prepared on the floor.

Scraps of food, any residue from spattered oil, and mysterious trails of sugar did not cover the floor. Dishes were not left uncovered in the fridge with the serving spoon still in place. The cheese did not smell like dirty feet.

I did not sit down on the bed with Betty and attempt to 'slip my arm' around her waist. I did not say: 'I really do not know how to tell you this, we are not going home. We are staying here.' I did not sit quietly while Betty screamed at me while our daughter watched, 'unable to comprehend this dark change in her father's demeanour.' I did not 'growl' like an animal. I did not say: 'I do not have to let you go home. You have to do whatever I say, and you are staying here. I did not push her over I did not shout: 'You are here for the rest of your life. Do you understand? You're not leaving Iran. You are here until you die.'

More important than anything else, I did not 'backhand' Mahtob in 'blind anger' so that 'blood spurted from a cut on her upper right lip, spattering into the dust'. I did not 'kick her sharply in the back'. I never 'pushed her aside roughly,' causing her 'tiny body to slam against a wall', making her 'cry out in pain'.

I did not strike Betty on the side of her head with my 'clenched fist'. I did not hold her hair and 'pound her again and again' on the side of her head. I did not slap her 'across the cheek with my open palm' and tell her: 'I am going to kill you.' I did not as Betty said, 'kick her in the back so viciously that paralyzing pains shot up and down my spine.' I did not 'become more methodical,' punching Betty in the arm, pulling at her hair, slapping her in the face, cursing all the time. I did not scream again and again: "I'm going to kill you! I'm going to kill you!" I never, ever thought of killing my daughter as Betty said; I never, ever thought of cutting up Betty into small pieces with a knife and of sending one of her ears 'back to her folks' as she put it. I did not tell her I would 'send the ashes of a burned American flag' along with her funeral casket.

Time and again Betty said I threatened her with death; saying over and over that I beat her and Mahtob, who always tried to come between us, to save her mother from my brutal attacks.

'Don't you worry,' Farik told me confidently, 'No one's gonna buy that rubbish. It's total nonsense.'

The book was massive hit.

It broke records in Europe and had soon sold more than a million copies in the US, rising to twelve million across the world. Betty was invited to give speeches at prestigious events and awards were heaped upon her. Even her local university gave her an honorary degree. In 1990 Betty was elected woman of the year and most courageous person of the year in Germany. A Dutch newspaper called her "Mother of all mothers". In 1992 *Not Without my Daughter* won the Dutch readers prize for book of the year.

I, meanwhile, was losing my mind. News about the book spread fast in Iran and it seemed as though many Iranians believed that the book was my fault, as if I'd somehow let down Iran. Malicious laughter and whispering followed me as I dragged myself to and from work. I tried to ignore it but it became impossible. I swung between rage, depression, heartbreak and embarrassment.

Letters from the Islamic Society arrived at work and home; they accused me of tarnishing the name of Iran. As the whisperers grew braver I was forced to protest my innocence at work, in the street, the markets - everywhere. I wasn't a wife beater! I loved my daughter more than anything on earth – I *had* loved my wife but now I just felt cold and hollow inside when I thought of Betty.

One day Farik came into my office, a worried expression on his face. He closed the door behind him and spoke with quiet urgency. "Listen," he said. "My cousin works for the cops. He has told me your name is on a blacklist; he thinks you're being followed by the secret police. If you don't leave Tehran now then you'll be stuck in Evin and tortured before being left to rot."

"That's crazy! I don't believe you," I protested.

"Trust me. I haven't seen it as bad as this since before the revolution with the SAVAK[3]. Things are really unstable at the moment, anything could happen."

He was right about things being unstable. The Imam, who was now 88, was unwell; his long life was coming to an end and, for the first time

---

3   The Shah's Secret Police

since the revolution ten years ago, a real sense of uncertainty was in the air.

A few days later, a young man entered my office without announcement. He was of slight build, looked to be about thirty, wore thick glasses and although he smiled with his mouth, the lines around his cold, dark eyes stayed immobile.

"I don't believe you are a bad person like your wife says, Dr Mahmoody," he said in a thin, sharp voice.

"Who are you?"

"In my line of work I have come across a great many different kinds of people who have done all sorts of things to harm the state - but you, Dr Mahmoody, are a special case."

I stayed silent and met his stare head on. He must be *Pasdar*, I thought. I had wondered how long it would be before they came. "I have patients-" I eventually began.

"I feel sorry for you," the thin man said, "It is a pity you could not control your wife."

"Look," I said, losing what little was left of my patience "What is this all about?"

"My job is to protect the Islamic State of Iran." He paused. "And to take whatever course of action would be of most benefit to the State."

At that moment another man entered my office and whispered something in the thin man's ear. "Duty calls, but we shall talk again Dr Mahmoody." He left without another word.

What was I mixed up in? What on earth was going to happen to me now? This was the last thing I had expected when Betty left – to end up as an enemy of the State.

Now fully paranoid, and on Farik's advice, I made amateurish attempts to check whether I was being followed. I stopped walking down the street and turned around suddenly as if I'd forgotten something at the office. I searched the reflection of the street behind me in the glass of office and car windows.

I quickly discovered that two men were following me wherever I went. They weren't making much of an effort to disguise the fact – after all, where could I go? There was nothing I could do to shake them off. My nerves grew increasingly raw as time went on. They could have picked me off the street anytime they liked, it could happen any moment, day or night and I would find myself being asked searching questions in an Evin prison interview room, being asked to confess to goodness knows what.

I paced my apartment at night, unable to sleep. Why had I been so stupid? Why had I ever wanted to come back to this? I'd had everything I wanted in America and I'd thrown it all away – for what? Now here I was, caught up in international politics, me, a middle-aged, short dumpy man with thick glasses! The thought was so ridiculous that I coughed out a scornful, "Hah!"

Life carried on but I just went through the motions. Two men in a car were always outside my apartment when I returned home and I usually spotted a familiar face waiting near the hospital doors as I arrived for work.

Farik came into my office one morning. "Have you heard?"

I looked at him miserably, thinking 'What now?'

"No," I replied, "What is it?"

"The Imam Khomeini has had a heart attack, he's mortally ill. The chief physician is with him now."

"He's being brought here?" I asked incredulously.

"No, he's at the clinic near his home. I've heard that there's no hope but that's not being made public right now. They've announced that they're 'optimistic'."

Farik always amazed me with his acquisition of knowledge; he really did know the spies and gossips better than anyone.

While I fretted about my future, Khomeini's supporters and enemies started to draw their battle lines as the founder of the Islamic government hovered on the brink of death. There was no obvious successor, certainly no one with the same stature waiting in the wings. Would anything change? I, like many others, feared that the nation's surviving rulers would want to become stricter, to tie down the people, making sure there would be no threat to them. I didn't think this would bode well for me.

That night the local TV news channel said there had been some complications, asking the nation to 'pray for the Imam'. This was enough to send rumours of his death flying through the city. The security forces were put on a state of alert, borders, airports and international telephone lines were all closed down.

When a second heart attack finally sent the Imam on his way that June night, the nation's most powerful politicians, who had gathered in the clinic, wept with the doctors and the family. All of them were mindful, however, that they needed to ensure they would be able to maintain control of the nation after his passing.

By early Sunday morning the streets were already filling with people. I spotted many war veterans among them; as the war had started almost from the first day of his rule, they held a particular affinity with the Imam. Meanwhile, revolutionary guards were mobilised and when I switched on the radio, every station broadcast recitations of the Qor'an until 7am when a weeping announcer read: 'The lofty Spirit of Allah has joined the celestial heaven.' The government declared five days of national mourning. Apart from essential services, everything was closed.

The country released its grief as one. People poured out into the streets. Hundreds of thousands of Iranians from all over the country travelled to Tehran to mourn and attend the funeral.

The government warned people to stay away from the official residence. They feared that the two million people on the streets would succumb to mass hysteria. Despite the hundred-degree heat, crushing mobs created an impassable sea of black for miles as they wailed, chanted and rhythmically beat themselves in anguish.

Fire trucks had to be brought in to spray water on the crowd to provide relief from the heat, while helicopters were flown in to ferry the eight killed and more than four hundred injured to hospital; we worked flat out.

It was amazing. People who had only recently been complaining about the privations caused by war and the poor state of the nation were weeping as though their own child had been lost to them.

On the day of the funeral, TV pictures broadcast from helicopters made it look as though Tehran was sinking in a great pool of black oil as two million mourners congregated and crushed each other in tumultuous grief.

Iranian officials aborted Khomeini's first funeral, after crowds stormed the funeral procession, nearly destroying Khomeini's wooden coffin to get a last glimpse of his body. At one point his body actually almost fell to the ground, as the crowd attempted to grab pieces of the death shroud. It was eventually rescued by helicopter.

Meanwhile, although I hadn't been charged with anything as such and hadn't heard from my mysterious visitor again, I decided to take Farik's advice and leave Tehran, to move to a new city and lie low for a while. The men who had been following me had vanished in the run-up to the funeral and it was easy enough for me to slip away during that chaotic time. After an emotional goodbye to my sister I set off for the city of Arak.

The war with Iraq, which everyone on all sides had had more than enough of, was finally coming to an end. As I travelled I noted with my own eyes how it had done such huge damage to our economy and the living standards of ordinary Iranians. I saw veterans who had been crippled by mines and missiles, or who had been blinded or robbed of their breath by chemical weapons. As a country we owed them a tremendous debt and would need to care for hundreds of thousands of these former soldiers for decades to come – for the rest of their lives.

The towns I passed had been swollen by refugees from the border, 1.6million of whom had been made homeless, not to mention the hundreds of thousands of jobs that had been lost thanks to the destruction of factories, roads, refineries, government buildings, ports and bridges. We were on our own as well; we couldn't count on any help from outside nations to rebuild our country. It would be an understatement to say that tough times were ahead.

Although Arak, a cold dry city, Iran's industrial heart, is home to half a million souls and is therefore a large city by Iranian standards, there's really not that much to recommend it. It was modern by Iranian standards, barely two hundred years old, but it had grown fast, thanks in part to an oil refinery and pipeline as well as a modern railway. It's recently become infamous for housing a heavy water production plant used as part of Iran's struggle for nuclear power.

It was in Arak - through a friend of Farik - that I managed to find work at the city hospital where I sank into blessed obscurity.

I didn't dare approach the authorities for fear of drawing attention to myself. Going to America was, for the foreseeable future anyway, just a pipe dream. I knew I had to bide my time and hope that things would change enough for me to be able to contact Betty and Mahtob.

But Betty wasn't done with me yet...

Betty's story was turned into a Hollywood feature film starring the diminutive Oscar-winning actress Sally Field. Released days before the start of the First Gulf War in August 1991, *Not Without My Daughter* also starred Alfred Molina, who is the total physical opposite of me, a tall, muscular man with a bushy beard (he also played super-villain Dr Octopus in *Spiderman II*). He portrayed me as a brutal, disturbed, menacing and violent monster.

The film, like the book, portrayed all Iranians as culturally backward, dirty and cruel (we shower once a year, eat cockroaches and worms, most husbands beat their wives and children, we're inbred and so on). It was perceived by Iranians to be an anti-Iranian diatribe that fitted well with popular American feeling at the time and played a small role in helping to maintain support for the war with Iraq in the Gulf (Iraq now knew, like Iran, that America could quickly change its loyalties and turn former allies into enemies when it suited them).

Although the film did well at the box office, it received some terrible reviews in the USA. Vincent Canby, writing in the *New York Times* on January 11 1991 said:

'"Not Without My Daughter," a title that sounds like a line from a travelling salesman joke, is the first major clinker of the year. It's a seriously intended movie that goes grossly comic when it means to be most solemn. It's a tale of mother love and freedom that is both mean and narrow.

The source material is the true story of Betty Mahmoody, an American woman married to Moody, an Iranian doctor who lived in the United States for 20 years. In 1984, against her better judgment, Mrs. Mahmoody went to Iran with her husband and their small daughter, Mahtob, for a two-week visit with his family.

Once in Teheran, Moody changed, or, as the movie portrays it, he reverted to his more primitive personality. Having sworn on the Koran to protect his wife and daughter and to see them safely home again, he decided to remain in Iran to work for the success of the Ayatollah Khomeini's fundamentalist Muslim state.

Mrs. Mahmoody was told that she could leave, but that her daughter would have to stay. As the title spells out, she would have none of this. After 18 months, she and Mahtob finally escaped with (according to the film) the help of some kindly Kurds and a rich Iranian, who talks fondly of the good old days.

"Not Without My Daughter" probably didn't set out to be biased against all things Muslim, but when such a complex, loaded subject is treated so witlessly, the effect is certainly bigoted.

The movie was written by David W. Rintels and directed by Brian Gilbert, mostly on locations in Israel. Sally Field stars as Betty who, as she plays her, is a sincerely unpleasant, rather stupid woman.

In Paris, she would be the type of tourist to insist on eating at McDonald's. In Teheran, absolutely everything earns her complacent disapproval. With just a few minor changes, "Not Without My Daughter" might have become a hilarious in-law joke.

On their arrival at the Teheran airport, Betty, Moody (Alfred Molina) and Mahtob (Sheila Rosenthal) are overwhelmed by the members of Moody's family. The in-laws descend on them like an attack force out of "Lawrence of Arabia," the harpy-like women, who are dressed in black chadors, wailing as if for the dead.

Poor Betty herself is required to put on a chador. It's the national dress code. She obliges but feels compelled to ask Moody: "Are they so afraid of women's sexuality? I know it's a different culture and all, but I still don't understand it."

From the time that she and her family arrive in Iran, until she finally flees, the scales drop from Betty's eyes with numbing regularity and thunderous booms.

The once charming Moody becomes withdrawn. He breaks the oath he swore on the Koran. He beats up Betty. He lies. One of the many last straws is when he is rude to his American mother-in-law when she telephones from the States.

The movie is so clumsily directed that nothing rings true, neither the idyllic scenes of Betty's family's happiness, which open the film, nor the horrors of fundamentalist fervour. The Iranian revolution appears to have taken place mostly to make life miserable for the insufferably superior Betty.'

This seemed to me, to be a skilfully written review - not just of the movie but of the book as well. Owen Gleiberman, writing in Entertainment Weekly, January 19, 1991 agreed: 'A nightmare in every sense of the word.

SAYED MAHMOODY

In this atrocious political- exploitation thriller, Betty Mahmoody (Sally Field), an ordinary middle- class woman living in Alpena, Mich., with her Iranian-born physician husband and their young daughter, agrees to take a trip with the family to Iran. It's the mid-1980s, and Betty's husband (Alfred Molina), stung by the racism he has encountered in the United States (and inspired by the resurgence of Islamic fundamentalism under the Ayatollah Khomeini), undergoes a sudden, fanatic reconversion to Islam, insisting that the family now remain in Iran and that Betty start conducting herself like a good Iranian wife (i.e., like a loyal servant).

The filmmaking is so crude that we aren't given an inkling of the husband's psychology. Overnight, he simply turns into a wife-beating, teeth-baring thug. And so even though the movie is based on the real Betty Mahmoody's 1986 account of her ordeal, it seems to be saying: Betty's husband may have lived in America for 20 years, but deep down he was always one of them. The movie takes the story of Betty Mahmoody's escape from Iran and turns it into a demagogic anti-Iranian horror show-one that, in the current climate, can easily feed anti-Iraqi sentiment as well. It would all be worth getting mad over were the film not so plodding or so obvious in its tactics.'

...

I was in my little claustrophobic office in the hospital when I received an unexpected visit. Sensing movement, I looked up and, standing in the door was a broad man in his fifties. He smiled warmly.

"How is life then Dr Mahmoody?"

"Well, thank you."

"May I?"

"Of course, please come in. Who-?"

'I am from the Ministry of Culture and Islamic Guidance.'

My heart sank. Back in the 1930s the Ministry of Culture and Islamic Guidance had been a small department, but since the Revolution it had become a pernicious, all-powerful body that had absorbed departments such as the Ministries of Tourism, Information, Art, Science and Higher Education. It still maintains a hand in everything that Iranians read and see, anything in print[4] or on screen and will knock on the door of any new emerging talented artist from any field to provide them with the 'appropriate guidance' that befits the Islamic Revolutionary State.

Putting Ministry before words such as Culture and Art always seems to me to turn them into something sinister sounding but in this case it really was true. It's the perfect realisation of George Orwell's Big Brother.

One of its roles remains to: 'Conduct research works on the propaganda campaign of international media and becoming familiar with their techniques and the ways to counter their measures if needed.' It was this responsibility that had caused them to come for me.

"I see," I said.

'Do you watch Iranian cinema, Dr Mahmoody?'

"My work keeps me busy..."

Thanks to the Ministry for Culture and Islamic Guidance, filmmaking really was a fine art. If you want to make a film then you have to go through the official channels, there's no other choice – and if they decide to let you make your movie you have to hand it over to them for editing before it's shown in public.

Directors have had to find very creative ways to escape the scissors of the Ministry for Culture and Islamic Guidance with a lot of shots and talks about birds and flowers in place of love scenes, for example. They've also produced entire films based on a single metaphor or very simple stories with very simple dialogue in the hope that audiences will add depth and meaning to what they are watching.

I recall one film about a lost girl who, after wandering the streets of Tehran turns to the camera and says 'I don't want to be in this film anymore,' and then goes home. For some reason, films like these sometimes won win the plaudits of a handful of highbrow international film critics and always won lots of awards, but most Iranians preferred bootlegged modern Western films.

At that time, Iranian films all seemed to be about triumphant missions carried out in the war. I'll never forget seeing the Iranian equivalent of the film *Top Gun* that features bombing raid after bombing raid on increasingly

---

4 But not this book.

incompetent Iraqi generals and with no discernable plot. Other 'romances' featured handsome but tortured young men beating up tubby thugs to impress their sweethearts – usually beautiful girls fallen on hard times and had, all too often, lost their 'honour'. Once you'd seen one, you'd seen them all.

The only other kind of Iranian films, a more recent trend it has to be said, the ones that survive the censor's scissors and sometimes made it to international film festivals, show poverty and despair in rural Iran.

If, by some miracle the film successfully passes though the Ministry, they then still decide where and when it can be shown – in which towns, cinemas and to whom. And people say film making in Hollywood is a tough business.

'I see', the man said. 'Do you know that many creative directors of Iranian cinema have, until recently been held virtual prisoners in their own homes and stopped from working?'

I said nothing.

"Times change. There is a great interest in cinema now. In American films, too."

I raised my eyebrows in surprise. I had noticed significant changes after the Imam's passing. To help rebuild Iran, the government was once more encouraging foreign investors and, I had noted with eager interest the newspaper reports that travel restrictions to other countries were going to be eased.

"Not to be shown to the public of course but they are being studied and we will use films to inspire the people to rebuild our great country. I know that many Iranians own old VCRs and that there are many dealers in American pornography, action films, even European art-house films as they're called."

"What-?" I began.

"I am coming to my point now, Dr Mahmoody. There is one American movie that has reached a - certain notoriety - shall we say? Amongst those who dabble in this illegal viewing."

I shrugged.

"Can you guess what it is called?"

"I think I know," I said, looking down sadly.

"Now, now, Dr Mahmoody. Don't look so sad. After all, our citizens are seeing this movie as a comedy."

"Excuse me?" I asked, incredulous.

"Yes, the movie is so bad, the people are laughing at it!"

"Well, I agree, it's –" I stopped but too late.

"It's alright Dr Mahmoody, if it had been me I would have wanted to have seen it as well. I will not chide you about such a small matter. But there is something that you can do for us. How would you like to return to Tehran?"

"I would like that very much."

"Wonderful! So that's settled then."

"Um. What is?"

"Well, the Ministry would like you to move back to Tehran and teach at the university."

"Medicine?"

"Well yes, I suppose if you like. But what we'd really like you to do is to teach our students about how the West plays tricks on its people about Iran. I'd like you to show people this film and to explain to them the truth, so that they will never believe their eyes when dealing with the West, so that they will understand how the Western government uses Hollywood to lie to its own people as well as to people across the world."

"I'm not sure I can do such a thing."

"But Dr Mahmoody, you are an intelligent man – you saw what was wrong with that film. Who better to explain than the very man that this film is supposed to be about. I mean look at you, forgive me, but you're no Alfred Molina, that's for sure!"

At this he laughed. I just continued looking perplexed, puzzling over how odd my life had become, how out of my control things always seemed to be.

Still, I was delighted that Betty had sold the film rights to her book. The thing that had nearly destroyed me was now my saviour. The film made it really clear to many Iranians who had accepted the word of Betty's book (often without reading it) that Betty's story was deeply flawed. The shrewd man from the Ministry wanted to seize this opportunity to drive the message home and turn it against the West.

I gratefully returned to Tehran and, after a joyful family reunion, I rented an apartment between the hospital and the university and busied myself with my work.

I dared to hope again. If I did a good job, and if I was welcomed back into society then maybe, just maybe I could find Mahtob in America and write to her, to let her know that I loved her, that whatever had gone before I was sorry for – I knew I would probably never convince her about her mother's account. I was sure Betty would have polluted those few happy memories of me that still remained.

For the first time since Betty left, I approached life with some optimism. I looked often at the watch that Mahtob had given me and dared to smile in the hope I would see her again.

I watched the film several times and, with the help of a wild-eyed film director who had until recently been banned from working, we cut together a sequence of scenes which I wanted to show the students I was expected to teach.

Walking to the lectern for the first time and standing there with the large screen behind me, well, I was feeling pretty shaky.

Before me were fifty-five of Iran's most intelligent young minds. Every year, almost one and a half million Iranians take part in university entrance exams and only about 300,000 get in. Every year, at the end of August, it's all everyone talks about. Those who are successful become celebrities in their families. Those who aren't think it's the end of the world. Some commit suicide. Needless to say, those who make it take their education very seriously indeed.

The number of women present in the lecture hall surprised me but, thanks to the war, they'd been encouraged to join Iran's universities to replace the hundreds and thousands of young men who'd given their lives in that senseless conflict.

I wondered how these young women, who found themselves in an ever-so slightly more liberal society in the wake of the Imam's death would react to my story. I also wondered how I would cope emotionally with showing the film while talking about my past. My most important audience member was the man from the Ministry who smiled as I stood up to talk. If his smile was intended to reassure, I didn't feel it.

I took a breath and began.

CHAPTER TWO

THE RETURN

August 3, 1984

"You'd better get ready," I said, putting my book down and checking my watch. Betty nodded and searched for her purse before making her way unsteadily towards the toilets at the back of the plane.

I looked at Mahtob. Our daughter was fast asleep, her mouth slightly open, her head turned away from the window of the Boeing. Outside, dawn was about to break.

Mahtob was so incredibly beautiful, a constant marvel. She slept the sleep of the innocent, as only children can. As I watched her I had a little flutter of panic. Had I done the right thing? Although Betty seemed much better, much stronger, I couldn't be absolutely certain. Of course now it was too late, we were on the plane and our fate was already sealed.

I nervously checked my pocket for our passports, visas and my medical papers. I hadn't been back to Tehran for over a decade, only twice in two decades. Since that last visit Iran had undergone a religious revolution before being invaded by Iraq and drawn into a long, miserable conflict.

Like all Iranians I watched the revolution unfold with fascination. Only a few years earlier, I'd believed like most that the Shah was omnipotent and irremovable, and then suddenly he was out. Now, for the first time in centuries, it felt as if the people had finally taken control of their country and were steering it in a new and unexpected direction. Of course, not everyone was happy about this - America, for one. Unfortunately, Iran quickly went on to sour its already rocky relationship with the USA with the US embassy hostage crisis.

I'd lived in and loved both countries. I'd been raised in Iran by my respected and well-connected family and educated as a young adult in the West before going on to spend the next twenty years of my life in America. I spoke English as well as I spoke Farsi and I felt more American than Iranian. I regarded the US as my home on all levels - socially and spiritually

If you'd told me just one year before that I'd be going to Tehran with Betty and Mahtob, I would never have believed it – never in a million years. Just one year ago, our relationship was as about as difficult and as complicated as it's possible for any couple's to be.

I looked out of the window, over the clouds coloured pink and gold by the dawn before my attention was drawn to my reflection in the thick glass. Until I'd met Betty, I'd all but given up hoping to fall and love, marry and raise a family. I did sometimes wonder what Betty had seen in me. I was middle-aged, balding, podgy, narrow-shouldered and short. I was also dependable, kind, caring and patient and I truly had fallen in love with Betty almost from the first moment I saw her – the day she became my patient.

A shaft of sunlight shone between the peaks of the Elburz Mountains in the distance. The sun seemed to be rising quickly, especially once the plane turned and flew towards it; shadows cast by the huge mountain range stretched for many miles.

I'd first flown back into Iran from England as a teenager, way back in the 1960s. I recalled that landing in Tehran was a very dramatic experience and started with a steep and bumpy dive, courtesy of the almost impassable mountains that bordered Turkey.

Anxiously, I turned and looked for Betty; she didn't like flying. She'd be reduced to a nervous wreck if the plane started jumping around now. I didn't want her to have to meet my family in such a state.

Betty was walking unsteadily back down the aisle, her hands palming the headrests as she went. She was wearing a dark green suit, dark stockings, glasses and a green scarf around her head. She looked uncomfortable and very, very tired. We'd been travelling for almost two days straight. I wondered whether she was starting to regret her decision.

But I had to come to Iran. My country desperately needed doctors to tend to the hundreds of thousands of men, women and children that had been affected by this senseless war with Iraq. Of course, I also could not wait to see my family. I had missed them so much, my dear sister especially in recent years, and I wanted them to meet my wife and my incredible four-year-old daughter for the first time.

Nevertheless, I nervously wondered, as I'd already done a thousand times before, what Betty would make of Tehran, of Iran, of my family.

I had warned Betty that since the revolution the Westernisation of Iran had all but stopped. Dress codes for women had been reintroduced. "I'm sure they're not that strict," I'd reassured her, "Iran is a very liberal country, more so than most people think, it's nothing like we see on the TV."

Betty looked at me with a nervous frown as she sat down and then jumped as the fasten-seatbelts light pinged on.

"What is it?" she asked anxiously.

"We're going to land," I replied.

"Finally," she answered, smiling nervously. She turned to check on Mahtob.

As soon as the captain had finished announcing our imminent landing, the engine whined and we fell through the air. An excited buzz rippled through the plane as passengers marvelled at our rapid descent.

Mahtob opened her eyes. She shared the same worried expression as Betty. I smiled. "Hello darling, it's alright, we're just about to land now."

Mahtob pulled her bright green bunny, which had half fallen off the chair, close to her. It was her favourite thing in the world; she took it with her wherever she could. With her free hand she reached across and Betty took her tightly by it.

"Don't worry," I said, "this is perfectly normal; we'll be on the ground before you know it."

Inside, I was nervous as they were. I was a stranger in my own land. I even spoke Farsi with an American accent. I was definitely a mixture of East and West, although I felt now as if I belonged more to the West. Everything I'd worked for was there. We lived in a large luxurious home beside a lake full of wild fish. I had a successful medical practice that provided me with an income of over $100,000 a year. USA was Home.

Iran was a land of distant memories. Had time softened those memories? Did I now romanticise my birthplace? Was it foolish for us to have come?

As the wheels squeaked on the rough tarmac, I looked at Betty and Mahtob and I told myself that as long as we were together, then everything would be okay.

CHAPTER THREE
ROYAL BEGINNINGS

By becoming a doctor I had followed in the footsteps of my mother and father who'd both cared for Allied troops brought to Tehran during World War Two. The Soviet and British armies had occupied the country after a series of short battles; the Persian Corridor was crucial for the shipment of war materials from Russia to the Western Allies in Europe.

At that time we lived near the Iranian/Iraqi border in the magical island city of Shushtar; surrounded by the Karun River which, according to legend, fed the Garden of Eden. More crucially for the Allies, this was Iran's only navigable river that emptied into the Persian Gulf.

Shushtar is a place of waterfalls, romantic mist, ancient bridges and temples that sit alongside modern houses and businesses. It was where the Allies brought their sick and wounded by the hundred - from India and beyond.

While Churchill, Stalin and Roosevelt met for the first time at the Tehran Conference of 1943 and debated Russia's role (the Germans had just been repelled at Stalingrad and Stalin, sensing profit in victory, promised to help the Allies), my father lost his fight against typhoid, a dreadful disease contracted from one of the hundreds of English patients he had been treating.

Whenever I pass by the English military cemetery in Qolhak Street, part of a beautiful tree-lined district of Tehran, I wonder whether any of those men had known my father, and whether there are any still alive who remember him, whose lives he might have saved.

I have no memories of my father; I was a baby when he died. I do not have many more memories of my mother; she succumbed to lung disease when I was eight and I was raised by my sister, Ameh. Fifteen-years older, Ameh was already married with children and lived in Khorramshahr, a wealthy, cosmopolitan town in Southern Iran; home to a major oil port and some of the most exclusive residential districts in the country. I lived there for ten years; a great city of bazaars, labyrinthine markets which were filled with tea houses and every kind of shop, even a post office; all of humanity teemed though its arteries - students and mullahs carrying books, ladies dressed in the latest fashion in bug-eyed sunglasses, merchants, beggars and running, laughing children.

As an Englishman's home is his castle, so is an Iranian's garden. Our lives played out in the walled gardens throughout the hot summers, gardens where we slept at night on camp beds, staring at the stars until we fell asleep – my sister and I never grew tired of this wonderful experience. Along with my cousins, I dipped my feet in the pond to cool down before and after prayers before splashing water on each other – a prelude to a chase until they, being younger by some years and therefore weaker, gave in and collapsed bracing themselves for the tickling frenzy to come.

Ameh did everything she could to make me happy; our kitchen table was a constant aromatic delight of saffron, mint, tarragon, dill, plums, lemons, apricots and roasting red peppers. The thought of the heavenly smells and that billowed from our house – braised duck, lemon-grilled chicken, lamb kebabs, along with the promise of saffron ice cream meant I always left class post-haste.

To Ameh's joy, I was a natural academic and I flourished in school. When I graduated, my cousin, who was studying in England, convinced Ameh that I should be allowed to join him. There was a question over whether I should try to get into Tehran University. This was where the best and brightest Iranians were sent and the entrance exams were notoriously tough with a great deal of competition. Those who were successful were bound for success in Iran. Although I was a good student, the lure of foreign lands seemed to me much more tempting.

The Shah of Iran, Mohammad Reza Pahlavi, who had taken power from his father after the Allied invasion, encouraged young Iranians who did not go to University in Tehran to study abroad in an effort to Westernise Iran.

His picture was inescapable; it was everywhere you turned. The Shah was adorned with various titles such as The King of Kings, Centre of the Universe, Light of the Aryans; he was draped in military ribbons and peppered with jewels. Although he embraced the modernism of the West his regime remained barbaric. If the wrong person heard you make a joke about the Shah, the SAVAK would whisk you away and spend a week or two on your 're-education'.

After World War Two, Iran went through a tumultuous readjustment as the nation industrialised and pumped out millions of barrels of oil. Poverty was widespread and the Shah's policy of 'New Civilisation', which alienated Iran's ancient cultures didn't help, while the 'White Revolution' failed (his land reform programme, much-trumpeted by Washington). Iran could no longer feed itself.

Socially, Iran was a confusing place; new consumerism and American influence produced many curios, from miniature golf courses and fast-food restaurants to bowling alleys (ironically this working class sport became the hobby of choice for many rich Iranians), heated public pools, ice rinks and modern cinemas which showed risqué Hollywood movies. The Swiss-educated Shah spoke French better than Persian and he often made embarrassing grammatical errors. He curtailed Islamic festivals, persecuted mullahs, tried to make Iranians forget parts of their culture he didn't like and spent $200 million on a festival to celebrate 2,500 years of Iranian monarchy.

Fortunately for me, I had no need to fear the Shah or poverty. We were wealthy merchants and so my sister was happy to be able to send me to study English in London as soon as I turned eighteen.

It was a real thrill for me, a naïve young Iranian, to arrive in such an alien metropolis – and completely formative. I had spent most of my life living in the strange world of a Middle Eastern culture that extolled the West. Suddenly I was in the 'real thing' and I soaked it up – literally as it rained incessantly from the moment I stepped off the plane. The cab driver that transported me into central London assured me that this was normal and I should expect to see very little sun while I was in England.

I soon forgot about the wet weather, however as the sights, sounds and smells of London were all so alien, even the English language was different from what I'd so far learned in Tehran. I heard words such as 'cool', 'hip', 'man' and 'far out' and tried to use them for a while, but even I realised I sounded ridiculous.

I suffered no overt racism worth mentioning; I wasn't the only fee-paying international student and my pale-skinned classroom colleagues treated me like an exotic curiosity. Iran was still very much an enigma to them;

this was still before the Shah leapt to international infamy as an extravagant wastrel of our oil economy, and as an oppressor of his own people.

My school was on Kensington High Street and once the initial part of my English education was completed, I opted to study Civil Engineering at the City of Westminster College, just across town. News about the East-West space race – especially about who would be first to conquer the moon - was everywhere and I quickly fell in love with the idea of being part of it. To me, the most exciting thing on earth was about how to leave it for the great unknown. Space travel was the ultimate adventure and surely where humanity's future lay. All my efforts at studying were designed to lead me to anything, absolutely *anything* to do with the Gemini and Apollo programmes.

"Your efforts might be better directed with us here on earth rather than up there in space Mr. Mahmoody," one teacher reprimanded me as he brought me back to reality with a well-aimed stick of chalk. He knew only too well what I was daydreaming about: walking on the moon.

I'd been writing dozens of letters to every company I could find that had anything to do with NASA, asking - well begging really - for a job. There were lots of opportunities for budding scientists who were prepared to work for peanuts. But, after months of space-like silence, I had come to think that America might as well be on the moon as far as I was concerned.

I was on the verge of giving up all hope when a cream, creased envelope with a blue airmail sticker clattered through the brass letterbox and fluttered down onto the welcome mat. The letter's stamp, which was of John Glenn (the third man to orbit the earth in space), was American. I tore at the envelope with shaking hands.

The company informed me that they had won a contract from NASA who'd asked them to design the release mechanism for the separation systems of first the Gemini, then the Apollo rockets.

There were several positions open for ambitious young engineers who were prepared to toil away in their laboratories every waking hour for very little financial reward. If this was amenable to me, the letter told me, and if I was prepared to finance my travel to the USA, then they'd give me a job.

I looked at the address. Missouri. I repeated the unfamiliar sounding word over and over and then searched out an atlas. It was pretty much slap bang right in the middle of the USA.

Although I needed my sister's permission, nothing would have stopped me from going. I would have swum the Atlantic.

Ameh was delighted for me, although her heart was heavy at the same time.

"First England and now we lose you to outer space," she told me sadly over a terrible phone connection. "Don't forget us here will you, my brother?"

I think she realised then that I'd really and truly left home. I think now that she believed I'd never live in Iran again. She knew that the sort of opportunities that awaited me in the USA were unimaginable to most Iranians, and so she let me go to the USA in more than just the practical sense.

Talking to Ameh was painful. I missed my family, my home, the sights, sounds, smells and tastes and it hurt my heart to think of it. I remain convinced that - for Iranian men especially - the ties to home are so strong that they threaten to reel you in at any moment. In some way I survived being so far away for so long by forcing myself to forget about home and to focus on my studies and work.

This was made easy for me in the USA. As soon as I arrived in Missouri in the spring of 1964, I had no time to think. I was put straight to work, and that suited me just fine. My bosses expected me to toil away like a fanatic on their project, which I did. I was immensely proud to eventually earn a place on the team that ensured that the retro-rockets would separate the Apollo craft from its solid fuel boosters.

We watched almost every moment of the eight-day mission to the moon and back, barely sleeping. I barely breathed during the launch and in the run up to the separation. The explosive bolts blew exactly as we planned at every stage – just $1/8000^{th}$ of a second after the scientist in ground control pushed the button. As the various inter-stage parts of Apollo tumbled back to Earth I breathed a little easier until, finally, the landing craft was orbiting the moon. I think we sometimes forget just how incredible this achievement was – we had sent a man to the moon using less computing power than a mobile phone. So much was down to timers, electronics, physics and mechanics.

I like to think that I helped NASA put a man on the moon and although it said 'USA' on the side of the rockets, people from just about every nation helped to send first Gemini and then Apollo into space.

The few hippies I saw in the States at this time looked to me like a cross between the bejewelled Shah and Sinbad the Sailor. And the women! Such princesses with their long hair and their short dresses; gyrating as they danced to the Beatles and then, more raunchily, to the Rolling Stones. And then Ursula Andress appeared in *that* bikini as James Bond made his cinematic debut in *Dr No*.

It was a frustrating time for me as, even though I went to my first 'happening', I was too shy to talk to anyone and too wary of drink and smoke to even contemplate the idea, so remained a resolute and lonely 'square'.

My edges rounded a little as the months passed. Like many short and unattractive men I found a way to fit in by using humour and I became a bit of a practical joker, often making myself the butt of the joke and imitating the new, exciting and fashionable British comedians of the day such as Peter Cook and Dudley Moore - as well as the wonderful Peter Sellers and old Goon Show records (much of which I barely understood).

There was a real buzz in the air; social and political upheaval rippled across the globe – the Cold War was heating up as Alan Sheppard was blasted into space hot on the heels of Yuri Gagarin, and John F Kennedy gave his inaugural address just before the Berlin Wall split Germany.

Kennedy was assassinated the day Duke Ellington and his big band were due to play in Tehran as part of his extraordinary tour of the Middle East. Later that same year, 1963, the Ayatollah, Iran's spiritual leader decreed: "The Shah must go!" Thousands answered his call and filled the streets of Tehran only to be torn apart by the guns of the Immortals (the Shah's Royal Guard, named after Xerxe's ten thousand elite warriors).

The Shah had the Ayatollah placed under house arrest before he left Iran for Europe, although not through choice as he came to live in exile in Paris via Turkey and Iraq. With the Ayatollah's ostracism, the seeds of the most original revolution of the twentieth century had been sown – but it would take another fifteen years of cultivation before they bloomed.

A feeling that something was still missing from my life followed the elation of being part of the wonderful experience of getting man as far as the moon.

I enjoyed the professional company of my colleagues but I still lacked real friendship outside of work – and of course the company of a woman. During those first frenetic work-heavy years, I'd been absorbed into and had come to love the USA without even noticing – and I still had so much to see.

Like millions of other immigrants, I considered myself to be just as American as the next person and had no desire to go back to Tehran any time soon.

Once the moon mission was over, I took time out to think about what to do next. I missed my parents. They would have given me guidance. I know if they had been alive I might have seen advice as 'interference' as many of my young colleagues did – but they were lucky to have both parents alive to interfere.

As I thought about my mother and father, I came to realise that I wanted to pursue a more humanitarian career, the most honourable profession there is, the profession of my parents: medicine.

It took me a while to find somewhere that would take on a 30-year-old intern but once I get my teeth into an idea, I don't let go and I eventually enrolled at the University of Health Sciences in Kansas City. After graduating, I carried out my internship at Carson City Hospital in Detroit in 1974.

And that's when I met Betty Love.

Chapter Four
WELCOMING COMMITTEES

"*Da hee-jon*! *Da hee-jon*!" I turned in response to the cry of "Dear Uncle" and there to my joy, was Zia Hakim, one of my nephews running towards me through the crowded airport. I called out "Zia!" in delight, threw my arms wide and grabbed him in bear-hug.

"Uncle, you're crushing me!" he said in English with a laugh.

"Sorry! Zia, it's so good to see you!" I stood back appreciatively, "You look great!" I wiped tears of happiness from my eyes. Zia was tall and handsome, with a fashionably styled thick head of hair. He was dressed in a finely cut English suit and a dazzling white shirt.

"Not so bad yourself Moody," he joked, punching me lightly in my paunch. "This, I can only assume, is the beautiful Betty."

"Oh goodness, yes, I'm sorry. Darling, this is my nephew, Zia."

Betty looked happy, happy for me, that I was able to see my family at long, long last. Zia showed off his polished English to Betty, "I am so happy you came," he said. "How long have we been waiting for this day!"

He then looked down at sleepy Mahtob, who'd forgotten her tiredness and was smiling, amused by this tall and dynamic man. Zia pecked her on the cheek and looked up. "She's SO beautiful!" he exclaimed. "I can see she takes after her mother."

I chuckled.

"You won't believe how many people are waiting to see you outside," Zia said, "Passers-by think some big-shot is in town! They've been waiting for hours, come on, let's not waste any more time here and go to them."

"But we still have to get through customs," Betty said.

I nodded in agreement and wondered how Zia had managed to talk his way past the ferociously bureaucratic customs officers. I recalled he was, like many in our family, a natural businessman and fixer.

Twenty minutes later we stood, sweating and weary as the luggage inspector, a tall, thin man with an enormous hook-like nose went through each piece of our luggage. As he finished going through one of my cases he looked up at me and asked me what I was doing in Iran.

"I'm a doctor," I told him with authority. "I've come from the USA to work."

"Work? What work is this?"

"I'm an anaesthetist. I'm going to help treat our wounded brothers from the front line."

"This is not allowed," he said gesturing at a bag that was full of presents for my family. He called over other inspectors and they started taking part every single piece of our luggage, and started unwrapping gifts that were for my family.

"Look," Zia interrupted with no little desperation, "it's going to take you all day to do that. This man is my uncle, his whole family are waiting for him outside."

"And her?"

"That's his wife."

The inspector looked Betty up and down. I didn't much like his expression.

"Okay. We will be in touch. You can take a bag of clothes."

"And my daughter's toy."

The inspector looked at the bunny with distaste.

"*Befarma'eed.*"[5]

Our compromise agreed, I quickly completed the paperwork and we walked, double quick, out of the terminal.

"What was his problem?" Betty asked Zia.

"Things are different now in Iran, Betty," he replied. "I'm afraid anyone who has been or has connections to America gets a hard time, no matter which family they're from." He saw Betty's worried expression. "But don't

5 *Befarma'eed* is one of the most common words in Iran, which means anything from 'please take a seat', 'come/go,' 'speak/say/go on', 'please help yourself', and 'there you are'.

worry," he added reassuringly, it's just the cops and the bureaucrats, no one else really cares."

Zia steered us towards the exit, "This way," he said excitedly, pulling me forward. I saw a large crowd in the parking lot and it was with some nervousness that I suddenly realised that this was my entire family. I wasn't sure I'd even recognise some of my younger cousins, so long had it been. Shouts of joy erupted as they spotted us and began stampeding happily in our direction.

They were crying, kissing and laughing; everyone had brought flowers. I hardly knew which way to turn, Betty was soon overwhelmed with bunches of roses. Mahtob clung onto her so as not to get lost in the enthusiastic melee.

I couldn't hold back the tears of joy as I saw my sister, Sara Mahmoody Ghodsi, the family matriarch, known to everyone as Ameh Bozorg or 'Great Aunt'. Tall, broad and tenacious, Ameh had hardly changed in twenty years. Even though she was bigger than me, she leapt into my arms in a crushing embrace. My knees trembled, my back creaked and I tottered unsteadily. She released me just in time and stood back, to look at me, tears streaming down her cheeks. "My dear brother! How could you make us wait so long?"

Her husband, Baba Hajji, was about my height; he was dressed in a loose fitting grey suit. He remained slightly aloof, as was his way. He was related to a senior religious man and owned a very successful business. He shook my hand warmly, nevertheless, and smiled through his pointed white beard.

Ameh could barely speak for excitement as she greeted Betty and then saw Mahtob. She drew in a great breath and knelt down to get on Mahtob's level. "My goodness Betty, she is so beautiful!" she cried happily. All the women sighed as one as they looked at Mahtob with love and reverence.

"Let's not waste any more time at the airport!" Zia said, clapping his hands and directing everyone to the car park. A beautiful ten-year-old turquoise Chevy in immaculate condition and covered in flowers awaited us. The three of us squeezed into the back seat, Mahtob in the middle. "Everything okay, sweetheart?" I asked. She nodded and stared back at me. She looked pretty dazed and confused. "An early night, tonight, I think." I said and winked.

Ameh climbed in front with Hussein, her eldest son, who had the honour of driving us. It was quite hard to see out the windows but I could tell Tehran was busier than ever, the narrow sidewalks were unable to contain all the pedestrians and many walked in the street. Women wore Chadors, soldiers seemed to be everywhere, and cars, vans, buses and trucks vied for supremacy over the road in a never ending tooting, revving and screaming cacophony.

"Don't you worry!" Hussein shouted in English, "I'll get you back safely, this is just like New York!" He then reversed the wrong way down a broad one-way street

"Just try that on Fifth and Broadway and see how far you get!" I joked.

"It's rush hour and Friday prayers," Ameh said, "it's crazy, tens of thousands of people are all trying to pack themselves into the city centre."

"It's because the President leads the prayers," Hussein added, "along with the speaker of the house."

I looked at Mahtob. She was taking in the chaotic scenes quietly, holding her bunny close.

It took us about an hour to get to Ameh's home in an affluent suburb in Northern Tehran. Not much had changed. The Chinese Embassy was still next door. A fence made up of tightly-spaced iron bars ran round the house and we passed through two double-doors to get to the central courtyard, where a huge pile of shoes told me that a lot of people were waiting for us inside.

"What a welcome!" I said, pointing at the shoes. "The whole of Tehran is here!"

"Well not everybody is crazy enough to go to Friday prayers in the centre of town," Hussein said.

"My brother is much more important than any prime minister," Ameh added with mock seriousness.

She'd also booked in caterers and they were busy working over three sets of grills in the courtyard. The main hall was huge, larger than many people's houses back home and the floor was deep in layers of luxurious Persian carpets. Sunlight reflected off a rippling swimming pool in the garden; its blue water looked terribly inviting.

We were once again surrounded, although this time it was more sedate. My extended family were deeply impressed by Betty and Mahtob, they kept saying how beautiful she was and how fortunate I was and of course I nodded my head in agreement.

My sister took us to where we would be staying, in a room in a wing set apart from the rest of the building; it was almost as if we had our own house.

It was exquisitely furnished with dark hardwood furniture, white walls and a large double bed covered in brightly coloured cotton sheets. The bathroom's cool marble floor was deliciously cold. A large bath, shower, toilet and bidet were in the bathroom.

Gifts were presented to Betty and Mahtob, they were each given a gold bracelet and beautiful decorative *chadors*, Betty's was a light cream with apricot flowers, Mahtob's was white with pink rosebuds. Betty accepted graciously and Mahtob quietly thanked my sister for the gifts.

The scene downstairs could have been from a movie. The late afternoon sun lit the room with soft orange-yellow light. Children in brightly coloured clothes ran from room to room and in and out of the flower garden laughing and shrieking with happiness.

My nieces Zohreh and Fereshteh served everyone delicious, strong tea, which revived us no end. Then the caterers carried in the food; bowls of yoghurt, fruit, flat bread, rice, cheese, beans, salads as well as cups of fresh herbs including a mixture of mint and basil. There were spicy vegetable sauces and meat dishes, everything we could wish for; my sister had spared no expense and delighted in our cooing approval.

I could tell Betty was putting on a brave face. Her narrow skirt made it awkward for her to sit on the comfy cushions arranged across the floor; she looked hot and bothered but kept smiling as people asked her if she was feeling okay. Ameh assured her that she'd get a chance to rest soon and I could see the relief on Betty's face. Mahtob was watching the other children with fascination. My heart leapt with excitement of the thought of her playing with them and speaking a little bit of Farsi; I was sure she'd pick it up quickly.

Then Reza arrived with his wife. He'd also stayed with us in the USA. Betty's face lit up when she saw him. His wife Essey also spoke excellent English and so Betty chatted with them, relieved to be sitting with a familiar English-speaking face.

Betty was looking so tired, she wasn't used to large gatherings like this one; her own family was comparatively small. "Moody, I'm really tired," she said, "I've got a headache and need to get to bed. Mahtob should go too."

"Of course," I said, "there's a small bottle of aspirin in my hand luggage in our room."

A few hours later I joined Betty and Mahtob. Finally, the air was cooler and I was glad to see they were both fast asleep, under the moonlight that shone gently through the window. I kissed Mahtob gently, "I love you, Mahtob," I whispered before I undressed and climbed into bed and cuddled up to Betty. "How's your head?" I asked her.

"Better Moody."

"I love you, Betty," I said as I laid my head on the pillow.

CHAPTER FIVE

FINDING LOVE

Betty was in a bad way. Brought to hospital in an ambulance in a critical condition, she screamed in agony and terror, the result of pains that ravaged her head, causing her muscles to jerk; spasms which forced her to curl into a foetal ball.

I first saw her in a separate, darkened room in the hospital. Betty was in her early thirties, had blue eyes, medium-length brown wavy hair and was quite plump, with a round, child-like face.

Her doctor had previously prescribed Ativan (a strong, highly addictive anti-anxiety drug, the long-term use of which can lead to psychological problems from depression to delirium) and Dalmane (also addictive, an unpleasant and very powerful muscle relaxant which was supposed to treat the muscle contractions but can lead to muscle control problems). They weren't working anymore - now it was down to me.

Most of my colleagues suspected (because of the severity of Betty's condition) that a brain tumour was responsible but one of them asked me if I could help bring the spasms under control.

Before I became an anaesthetist, I was a practitioner of Osteopathic Medical Therapy (OMT), a holistic approach to medicine based on the body's miraculous ability to heal itself. OMT places an emphasis on the body's musculoskeletal system, or how the body's interconnected system of nerves, muscles and bones interact. Practitioners use manipulative therapy to stimulate nerves and release muscle tension. It is effective in the treatment of chronic pain, especially migraines.

Betty lay on a firm orthopaedic table as I worked. Her muscles twitched and jumped as I pressed down on her with my palms and guided her body back into shape, feeling and kneading the large muscle groups, nerves and tendons, clicking and clacking bones and joints back into alignment. As I worked, I could feel her relaxing, although the pains in her head continued to hurt her terribly. Betty was understandably terrified; she'd overhead the doctors debating whether she had a tumour.

Finally, I cupped my hands under the lower part of her head, that part of the cranium that joins the neck, and steadily felt my way down the start of her spinal column. I gently lifted then pulled her head, twisted her neck ever so slightly and to my satisfaction I felt a firm 'click'. With that I had caused a sudden release of excess cerebral-spinal fluid.

Until then, Betty had been in too much pain to pay me much attention but now, suddenly amazed, she looked at me in wonder and said "I feel kinda great, I've got a warm feeling all over my body, I'm relaxed all over." She paused for a moment. "And there's no pain!"

No other woman had ever looked at me the way Betty did that day. I was not an attractive man - short and stocky, I was balding (it's nearly all gone now), a little overweight and I guess the kindest thing you could say about me was that I had a certain scholarly look, I was more mature than my fellow interns and I really went all-out to provide the most considerate and courteous care I could.

I did not often find myself in the company of women, especially not romantically. So I'll never forget how Betty's blue eyes sparkled at me in the darkened room, causing my throat to go dry. I developed a sudden stammer as I made my excuses and left, clumsily stumbling into a trolley on my way out.

Betty stayed in the hospital for a few days so the doctors could be sure she didn't have a tumour - which she didn't. She became my patient and I saw her regularly up until the day she was discharged, often popping into her room when I was passing or when I was just about to head home to see how she was getting along. She always had a bright smile. I tried not to stare but each time I looked at her, I was soon lost in her eyes.

Betty became my outpatient and saw me for a series of OMT treatments. One day I walked into my office to find her waiting for me. Puzzled, I asked her "I haven't forgotten an appointment, have I?"

"Not at all, I was passing and thought I'd say 'Hi'," she told me with a smile. We chatted until I had to get back to work. To my delight, she started finding any excuse to drop by the hospital to see me; usually just to make small talk, although once she brought her grandmother along for treatment.

I was very slow to take up the hint; I had all but given up on finding love and the penny only dropped when a friend accosted me in the corridor after Betty had stopped by: "She likes you, Moody. Time you did something about it, buddy."

Betty wasn't attractive in the traditional sense, but to me she was stunning. There was also something about her nature; she seemed so caring, gentle and just generally delightful to be around. Besides which, I found her interest in me tremendously exciting.

On her next visit, I found the guts to ask her out. Inexperienced in such matters, I complimented her on her perfume, Charlie; how I could still smell it after she had left the room. She blushed, smiled; there was some coyness there, I thought; was she encouraging me? Taking a deep breath, I asked if I might call her one night at home. To my delight she said yes. Emboldened, when we parted I leaned forward, to kiss her cheek – somehow we ended up pecking each other on the lips. I was electrified.

Shortly after we started dating I began my internship in Detroit where I planned to study to become an anaesthesiologist. I now had my green card, which allowed me to practise medicine in the USA.

I'd drive the three-and-a-half hours to see Betty every weekend when I wasn't on-call and she would come and stay with me when I was. I tried to do something special and romantic, no matter how small, for Betty every week, from mailing her love letters and little gifts to taking her and her two sons, five-year-old John and eight-year-old Joe on trips. When it was Betty's birthday I gave her a finely carved music box that played Brahms's 'Lullaby'. Inside was a delicate sculpture of a mother cradling her baby; "Because you are such a good mother," I told her.

Betty was wonderful. I thought my 39th birthday was a washout as just after Betty arrived to join me in Detroit I was called out by my buddy Dr Gerald White to an 'emergency'. Gerald was in on Betty's plan and when I arrived at the hospital he plastered a displeased expression on his face.

"Moody!" he said crossly, "There you are. What took you so long? We got Jim to come in instead. Go on home."

As I left, stomping my way back to my car, cursing my good friend, Betty was piling our house to the ceiling with Iranian food, folding chairs, wine, wine glasses - and all of our friends.

Best of all, Betty had made a cake in the colour of the Iranian flag with 'Happy Birthday' written in icing, and in Farsi. I was so surprised I could barely find my tongue to say thank you.

I'd never been so happy. That night, I told her for the first time that I was in love with her; that I had fallen for her the moment I'd looked into her eyes. Taking her hands in mine I said 'My heart is entirely yours,' and, with that, our destinies were sealed.

Chapter Six
SHOPPING WITH THE SECRET POLICE

At four o'clock the next morning we were woken by pounding on the door of our bedroom. "Time to get up, Moody!" Baba Hajji shouted in Farsi, "Time for prayers!" Outside, a loudspeaker crackled into life and the all-too-familiar sad, extended wailing sound called the faithful to their sacred duties.

'Oh gosh,' I thought, 'this isn't going to be easy.'

This was something I hadn't done in America but now I was back with my family I had to fall in line. Missing prayers in my sister's house was unthinkable.

Betty groaned as I got up. "I have to go for prayers," I explained.

"What the hell?" Betty said, waking.

"I'm sorry," I said and grinned apologetically, "but when in Rome..."

"Mmmph."

She was understandably unimpressed. With a yawn I slowly dragged myself up, washed my aching body and staggered out of our cool room into the hall. Even though it was 4am it was already warm; the temperature didn't drop much at night during August.

Once we were done I returned to bed and gratefully cuddled up next to Betty who was snoring softly. Unfortunately, Baba Hajii had other ideas and kept praying – very loudly. He read from the Koran out loud in a singsong chant that echoed its way through the large house.

By the time he left for work, Betty and I were wide-awake.

I went and woke Mahtob who had somehow managed to sleep through the commotion. "Did you have pleasant dreams?" I asked.

"Okay," she said, picking up her bunny and sleepily staggering towards the bathroom in that drunken way kids do.

Unable to resist, I asked her what she thought of Iran so far.

"It's nice, daddy," she said and thought for a moment. "I like Zia."

We showered, a wonderful cool relief from the heat. When I came out, Betty was up. "Do I have to wear the chador for breakfast?"

"Not indoors, not around the family," I said.

I left Betty to get ready while I went down to the kitchen to speak to Ameh. She greeted me with a beaming smile and a pot of strong, hot Iranian tea.

It seems strange to say it now, but I'd forgotten how much I loved Ameh. I was overjoyed to be having tea with her again; the luxury of being able to sit and talk to her face to face, to see her expressions and gestures was simply wonderful. Before, we'd end up shouting down a crackly phone line with a three second delay, which was enough to turn the simplest conversation into a real headache.

When Betty joined us I could see she was still exhausted. Ameh offered her sugar for her tea and Betty refused a bit tersely. Ameh threw me a worried glance; had she offended my wife? There's nothing more important to Iranians than providing the best possible hospitality. Upsetting a guest was unthinkable.

Speaking calmly in Farsi, I did my best to reassure Ameh. "Don't worry, all Americans are like this before they have their tea in the morning."

Ameh nodded, a sympathetic expression on her face, and then smiled at Betty who frowned.

"Why's she looking at me like that Moody? What did you tell her?"

"Just that you needed peace and quiet with breakfast."

Betty didn't look too pleased. Still, it was only the morning of our first day and we were still shattered after our marathon journey.

Our spirits were lifted when Majid, Ameh's youngest son, visited. "After today, there are many, many places in Tehran I must take you," he said good-naturedly in perfect English. "The Shah's Palaces to start and then no doubt, you would like to go shopping, presents for the family and for the little one," he added smiling at Mahtob who brightened at the thought.

I liked Majid's idea about shopping. If there was one thing I could do to brighten Betty's mood it would be to splash out on a few extravagant gifts.

"Excellent idea, Majid," I said in English, "Betty, why don't you call home and let your parents know everything's OK?"

She seemed strangely reluctant, I had no idea why but eventually she made the call.

This was going to be another long day; relatives near and distant arrived steadily throughout the morning, joining us for lunch and dinner. Men were met at the door with lounging pyjamas. They would change in another room before joining us in the main hall.

Ameh also had a supply of colourful clothes on hand for the visiting women. I had no idea who most of these people were and even I found it tough to keep talking, brightening only when they said they were going to leave. But this always turned out to be just another preamble for more conversations and even when we got them to the door they would talk for another half an hour or so – invariably another couple would arrive and so they would be dragged back in for another reunion. Such is the Iranian way.

Thankfully everyone had gone by the middle of the afternoon and the three of us were able to lie down for another sleep. We ate late in the evening, once Baba arrived back from work. Most things in the house were directed by Baba's presence, which was fair enough I supposed, as it was his import/export business that paid for everything. Baba was a very important figure in Tehran. His father had been a religious leader and his brother had recently died a heroic death in Iraq.

When we got up, Riza and Essy were downstairs. "The news is on," Riza said, "the English broadcast. You should see this Betty, you'll be amazed."

I could hardly believe it. It was like some savage, dark and surreal comedy. It started with ongoing war with Iraq and the handsome presenter rattled off a long list of Iranian victories. The cowardly enemy were vanquished time and again by our brave young men – it would seem without one single casualty on our side, something we all of course knew to be nonsense. The whole segment seemed to me to be a rallying call for more volunteers to join our 'victorious brothers on the front line'. It showed young men marching off to win their medals of glory. In reality of course I knew they would be facing the same conditions as millions of European men faced in the trenches during World War I. Charging the enemy in senseless attacks over a strip of desert only to be cut down by machine gun fire, mortars and mustard gas.

I said as much while the report played. I was soon stunned into silence, however, as the reports continued. Every other single news item was directed against America, which for some reason, had decided to side with Saddam against Iran. I wanted to switch it off so Betty wouldn't be unnerved.

"No," she said, without taking her eyes of the screen, "I want to see it."

Her face darkened as we watched. The reports said AIDS and junk food was killing thousands of Americans, that they were murdering each other over drugs and that the divorce rate was higher than it had ever been. In a way, none of these things were completely untrue but the way they were presented made America look like hell on earth.

Of course, my family, who had travelled abroad were liberal in their views of America, a country we all loved. We had a much better understanding of the global situation and Iran's place in the world than most other Iranians.

I was desperate to make sure that Betty understood she was extremely welcome and so I translated every conversation, every comment within earshot. Most of us spoke English all the time anyway; I preferred speaking English to Farsi.

I hated the thought that Betty wouldn't like my family and was equally worried that my sister would react badly if she realised that her hospitality was not going down as well as she hoped it was.

Despite this, from that moment forth, Betty became more critical of Iran and my family. She said the house was dirty, that there were bugs in the rice and that Ameh was gossiping about her.

We eventually went out to do some shopping. We were really looking forward to this part, the opportunity to buy exotic gifts from friends and relatives back home. Even a simple shopping trip was an adventure into a city that had almost doubled in size in the four years since the revolution.

Iran has about seventy million citizens, 90% of whom are - like myself - Shia Muslim. The remaining ten per cent is a heady mix of Sunni, Jewish, Christian, Zoroastrian, and Ba'hai minorities with Arabian, Kurdish, Turkish, Persian and many other backgrounds, all vying to make a living in one of the most chaotic countries in the world.

Tehran, home to almost ten million, was one big traffic jam. The whole city seemed to be under construction as builders raced to complete houses for the thousands arriving from the countryside everyday.

To my own apprehension, Revolutionary soldiers were ever present. They stopped cars indiscriminately, searching for antirevolutionary contraband such as drugs, American literature, or cassette tapes. Betty found the guns unnerving but I reminded her that every cop in America carried a loaded gun on his hip.

Far more worrying, I thought, were the Pasdaran, the new Secret Police. These were simply SAVAK by another name. My cousin Hussein had tried to warn me not long after I arrived but, having never had any trouble with the SAVAK, I'd brushed aside his warnings that the Pasdaran exercised a ruthless abuse of power. They could arrest whomever for whatever and send them to Evin prison; that dreaded cold fortress that sat in the shadow of the mountains on the edge of the city.

The Ayatollah created the Pasdaran very soon after he took power. During the revolution, the Shah's army – armed by the US – did nothing when the people rose up. First off, they found it very difficult, impossible in fact, to attack unarmed people who were peacefully chanting 'God is great!' Even the dreaded and much-trumpeted 'elite' Republican Guard did nothing.

The Ayatollah, who the Iranians call the Imam, understood why. They weren't loyal enough. Most of the Iranian army relied on conscription so the Imam asked for volunteers for the Pasdaran and gave them real power and a vested interest in keeping the Supreme leader in place no matter what.

People joined in droves; coming mainly from religious and working-class neighbourhoods, the foundation of the revolution. Anyone who joined had made a smart a move. Although they were initially formed to protect the Imam and the regime, they soon became much more proactive and went far beyond enforcing alcohol prohibition.

With the advent of war with Iraq, they formed their own air force and navy, and the now famous but quite small Qods Force (the Iranian version of the SAS). The Pasdaran made for fearless fighters and their strength grew as regular soldiers aspired to join them. They became better equipped and trained than the regular army – they held the keys to all of Iran's long-range missiles.

The supreme leader also made the Pasdaran the masters of the Iranian economy; to this day they handle Iran's natural reserves and exercise control over the volatile import-export market. If you want to do business in Iran then you have to do business with the Pasdaran.

And if you want to get on in Iran, as a young ambitious man or woman, then the best thing you can do is sign up for the Pasdaran. It's a job for life with fantastic chance for promotion and power with countless departments that control every aspect of Iranian society. They need to keep the Supreme Leader exactly where he is so they can continue to do this. It's one of the many smart moves the Imam made.

One of the Pasdaran's most public duties was carried out by a sub-group called the *Komiteh*, a national disciplinary patrol responsible for enforcing regulations on social behaviour.

They still drive through the streets today, their white patrol vehicles identifiable by the "K" in Persian on one side of the license plate. They make sure that unmarried men and women do not hold hands or walk together on the sidewalk, that storekeepers display in their shops large, glossy photographs of the nation's senior Islamic clerics and that women are 'properly dressed', which meant that their clothes covered their heads, chins, wrists and ankles.

The Komiteh has broad powers of arrest and imprisonment. Islamic law, as interpreted by the Government, means that officers can lock up people for the slightest offense. Even today, university students have told me that there are informers among them, and that these spies file reports about student drinking and romantic entanglements. Komiteh officers also work in certain hotels and restaurants, spying on the guests.

The irony was that it was female *Komiteh*, often referred to as the Fatemeh Commandos, who repressed their fellow womenfolk in this way.

On that day, Betty, Mahtob and I put all thoughts of soldiers and *Pasdar* to one side as we hit the markets and really started to shop. Our eyes had more than enough strange and exciting sights to keep us occupied and we pored over carpets, clothes, pillows and jewellery. It wasn't long before we encountered the unique hospitality, politeness and eloquence of the market traders.

Iranians are charming, welcoming and are far more curious than any cat. Although I understand the reasons why, it's a great pity that more people don't travel to Iran. We love meeting and talking to foreigners, and we're also very free with our help and advice (whether it's welcome or not).

Then, as now - thirty years on - most people in the West had a certain impression of Iranians. Before the revolution, most Iranians who travelled to the West were like me – wealthy, reserved and polite men and women from well-to-do, conservative families. All too often, our politeness was seen as aloofness.

Then, after the revolution, all the West saw of Iran were the crazy ones on the news images that were beamed out of the state-run TV stations, people that chanted 'Death to America' and who supported a fundamentalist regime that wanted to take the world back to the Dark Ages. They saw the men who took Americans hostage in the embassy crisis and they saw the Ayatollah Khomeini on TV every night ranting against the United States.

On the street, the truth is far, far removed from these extremists. Iranians tend to be so welcoming and hospitable that it often becomes embarrassing for most Westerners.

It's only our leaders and a small but determined minority that hate the West with a passion. We're just as friendly and happy to see foreigners move to our country, pretty much in the same way that America welcomed millions of immigrants via Ellis Island. We were just unlucky that an extremist minority had seized power in Iran.

Yes, the rest of the world has a one-dimensional view of our country – which is understandable - but most ordinary people remain keen to correct that whenever they get an opportunity. Despite the Islamic government and the Sharia Laws, Iranians are very quick to seize any opportunity to prove that they are just as sophisticated as Europe and America. Our taxi driver, a short septuagenarian with thick stubble and, worryingly, even thicker glasses that gave him owl-like eyes, was no exception. As he drove us to the market he quickly presented us with his life story and in no time at all we more about him than we would ever have wished.

I translated his Farsi for Betty as we drove.

He had six children; his eldest had been martyred on the front line. Like many Iranians he believed that the war would not have gone on so long were it not for America supplying both sides with weapons in recent years. 'But that is not your fault,' he said to Betty. 'Like me you are powerless to do anything about it. It's the crazy people in charge who seem determined to make life very difficult for us ordinary folk.' This sentiment has stuck with me in the years and decades to come. Time and again, ordinary Iranians have suffered thanks to the corruption and misguided judgements of their leaders. It's the same story across the world – it's always the little people that suffer.

Betty found his open criticism of the regime surprising and his fascination with life in America did something, I think, to repair the damage that the state run TV had done. I was delighted. Finally, we were seeing the real Iran.

At the end of the drive the driver made an over-the-top show of politeness. 'What's he saying?' Betty asked.

'He's saying we shouldn't pay him for the journey.'

'But why not?' she answered in surprise.

Again I translated.

'Because, he says, it was an honour for him to take us here and he feels that to take money from us would be an insult.'

'Oh.' Betty said, considering this for a moment. 'Well, if he really feels that way.' She smiled at him and said 'Goodbye and thank you very much, you're very kind.'

The taxi driver's mouth fell open in horror as Betty made to leave. He looked as though he'd been slapped across the face.

Betty saw his expression and stopped, half-in, half-out of the car. 'What is it?' she asked as I burst out laughing.

'It's okay,' I said through my laughter, ' this is the way things are done in Iran.' I turned to the driver and said, in the flowery language customary on such occasions: 'You are humbling us, you are more than worthy of payment, we insist.'

The driver's big eyes brightened. We were back on course again.

'It's not a big deal,' he said with a happy shrug, 'I am but a dwarf in your presence.'

'No you're worth it,' I said, pressing a note into his open palm.

'Now *you* are humbling *me*,' he said with a smile, reaching for change.

'No, you have earned it by the honest light in your eyes,' I replied, scooping up Mahtob, grinning and without taking the change.

'What on earth was all that about?' Betty asked.

'It's called *tarof*, and it's very special to Iranians. It's a way of making a polite exchange to judge how much hospitality both parties can afford to extend. Over time, it's spread into all areas of modern life. You may think that the English are famous for their politeness but that's nothing compared to the courtesy shown by Iranians. We take our role as hosts *very* seriously.'

'Sounds crazy to me.' Betty said with a smile. 'And exhausting.'

'Yes, it takes a bit of getting used to. If, for example, you offer someone dinner they will refuse, even if they are starving. The idea is to give the person who is making the offer enough time to gracefully bow out, so generally, the rule is to ask them the same question about three times. This is a very sensitive approach and is intended to help the poorest in our society – if for example they are unable to provide a decent meal for someone they've just met.

'If the person refuses the offer three times in a row, then it's okay to leave without paying or feeding them or making up the spare bedroom and so on. But don't worry, if you get it wrong, the shocked expression on the other person's face will set you straight soon enough and you can restart. But it can get very tricky sometimes, there are a few manipulative people who use *tarof* to their advantage.'

In this sense, tarof is sometimes used by less scrupulous Iranians to lull a business or love or political rival into a false sense of security before going behind their back. More sweetly, tarof also influences Iranian wedding ceremonies where the bride is asked three times if she wants to marry her betrothed. The groom, however, is asked only once.

Most Westerners find polite tarof hard to get to grips with – it sometimes feels a little bit like when a waiter asks you if your steak was cooked to your satisfaction and, even though it was raw in the middle, you feel obliged to say 'very nice' and even though the waiter has seen that you've left him no tip, he wishes you a pleasant evening and hopes to serve you again soon.

In business, tarof it is a type of polite negotiation during which two protagonists vie for an advantage. The Western way of doing business is more overtly aggressive and competitive and is, to Iranians, a back-to-front-way of doing things. Tarof extends to international politics as well, which probably explains a large part of the awkward diplomatic relationship between the US and Iran over the past half century or so – Iranians see Americans as loud, brash and ruthless while Americans see Iranians as sneaky, underhand with an almost supernatural ability to persuade them to open a door they had no intention of opening. It is hard for most Westerners to get to grips with tarof and it was certainly something that Betty most certainly did not understand.

To add to the confusion of Westerners, *gholov* - boastful exaggeration – runs alongside tarof and can be often seen on the international political stage. Currently the economy is in a tailspin, food, fuel and house prices are rising as is unemployment but that doesn't stop the leadership shouting from the rooftops that we are one of the ten most desirable countries in the world to live in. Much as I love Iran, I think that may be a prime example of gholov.

Even I am guilty of gholov when with other Iranians because it's expected and I try and make sure any new Iranian acquaintance understands that I am a doctor in as short a time as possible. I think Betty saw this as an unpleasant trait – which it may be – but it's not so different in the US, a country where people are very keen to know what you do for a living and how successful you are (which means finding out how much you earn) and they often share this information with, what seems to me, disarming eagerness.

When tarof collides with gholov then conversations can sound truly extraordinary with one party perhaps stating: 'Even though I have studied at Tehran and Harvard, drive a BMW and have fathered seven beautiful children, I am not worthy of your presence.'

The third national trait that's crucial to understanding Iranians, and the last one I shall mention here is *haq* - rights. Rights are deeply ingrained in the Iranian psyche. Rights are the reason why millions of men who beat themselves and weep during religious festivals during the month of Moharram, are consumed by paroxysms of weeping. They are in part crying for millennia-dead heroes, who like many European heroes from William Wallace in Scotland to Beowulf in Norway, died in their own pursuit of justice. Most of the tears fall because of the cruel injustices perpetrated to Iran and Iranians in living memory

This might mean the right to have nuclear power, or the rights we lost when the CIA backed coup of 1953 overthrew our then democratic government, the right to medicines and goods easily available elsewhere in the world but lost to Iran in international sanctions, as well as the basic rights for happiness, life, freedom and equality (unfortunately equal rights doesn't yet extend to women and the government of Iran still has no trouble in restricting a great many freedoms) – all of which are effected by these international issues.

Foreign powers, regrettably, often conspire to trample the rights of Iranians in pursuit of their own interests. Of course, the irony that the US helped overthrow the only democracy we ever had to replace it with a dictatorial monarchy is not lost on us, as they would now obviously like to see Iran become a fully democratic nation as opposed to an elected government controlled by religious leaders who have a god-given right to rule.

A full democracy would be fine, but our own leaders have had little history or experience with democracy, and there is always the danger that if ordinary men take power then they will start to exhibit dictatorial qualities not long after the people hand them control of the country.

Finally, another aspect that was especially confusing for non-Iranians to grasp in the 1980s, is that the Iranian sense of liberty is quite different to Western sense of liberty. To Iranians the first item at the top of the liberty list is being able to define one's own nation's future. There is no clearer demonstration of this than the 1979 revolution when the nation rose as one and freed itself from the rule of western-installed Shah.

Tarof, gholov and haq were alien concepts to Betty but they were thrown at her thick and fast from day one. Although I tried to explain she understandably didn't always get it – or even, in some cases, remember.

For example, when someone was particularly insistent Betty would walk away without paying, much to the shock and surprise of restaurateurs, merchants and taxi drivers.

This, I felt, had something to do with the very different approach to hospitality between the West and the Middle East. As usual, we both wanted to achieve the same things – in this case the appropriate payment for a service - but had very different ways of going about it.

So, as you can no doubt imagine, bartering involves a great deal of talking and repetition. As we wondered through the dark but colourful maze of the bazaar, passing shops that sold everything from precious stones to batteries, I soon slipped back into the old ways and really started to enjoy the lengthy but very friendly process.

Mahtob pointed at everything and everyone as I carried her, asking all sorts of questions. I answered her with delight and the three of us laughed often. It felt like we were really the happiest of families, it seemed as though Betty and I had left the bad times behind us in America.

We quickly found some stunning Persian carpets and in no time at all we found ourselves sitting in the Bakhtiari Brothers carpet shop sipping tea from little glass cups contained in metal frames as the merchant showed us dozens of dazzling carpets.

Drinking black tea – something Iran inherited from the British - during any negotiation or social setting is essential – it is never offered, always given and always drunk. After our second cup he invited us up a narrow set of stairs into a small attic where he kept the best of the best. As with all tribal rugs, they were hand-woven and imperfections in the patterns were clearly visible. Only God is perfect, after all. This one, made by Kurdish nomads, was almost a hundred years old and it had taken months to create.

We loved and wanted it and 'Oohed' and 'Aahed' over the patterns, colour and texture. Mahtob joined in happily and - after the necessary amount of polite negotiation – starting with the merchant wanting to give it away, we gradually worked towards a figure that was agreeable to both and I was able to say I had paid too little while he said he had sold it for too much. The money, though, changed hands and vanished into the merchant's robes with speedy aplomb.

I was now much happier. Betty was really fascinated and fell in love with the bazaar where she was treated like a princess. After every purchase you really felt like you'd made friends and got a bargain to boot.

Whenever Betty saw something she liked I opened negotiations and we ended up drinking a great deal of tea as we bought hand-embroidered pillowcases and picture frames.

Yes, we were really starting to have fun together for the first time when, after becoming lost in a particularly delicate piece of *tarof* negotiation on the edge of the bazaar, I turned and - to my horror - saw a Pasdar leaning of the window of a white pick-up, shouting at Betty.

Chapter Seven
FULL OF SURPRISES

I pulled up and got out of the car and looked around, my mouth open. I was in the middle of some woods and…well, I thought to myself, I had to be at the wrong address.

But just then Betty emerged from the tiny, tumbledown house, ran over and embraced me in a crushing hug. This was the first time I had been to her home; I knew she was poor, but this was a real surprise. Betty lived in this draughty miniature house with her two sons, Joe, who was nine and John, who was five, and two adopted daughters, Lynn and Lori, both fourteen.

She came from a poor family and had fallen pregnant very young. Shortly after we started dating, Betty told me she had just emerged from a disastrous marriage to a farm labourer and was working part-time at a car-parts factory that produced door-hinges; she survived largely thanks to benefits.

'A woman as wonderful as Betty shouldn't have to live like this,' I thought.

As we continued dating, I 'adopted' her family, bought presents for them and became a regular visitor at Betty's house. I took great delight at their pleased reactions when we went out on 'family' outings. I made sure I never forgot a birthday, holiday or anniversary. The first time I took us out for slap-up meal in a decent restaurant, the normally boisterous Joe and John suddenly became quiet. The civilised formality unnerved them; they simply didn't know the rules.

I hailed from the other side of the social divide and their poverty really brought home to me just how privileged I was. As I've already mentioned, my family were practically aristocratic and although we were by no means filthy rich we were still very wealthy. I'd never wanted for anything and now here I was, living on my own with no outgoings and a junior doctor's salary. It was very easy for me to provide for Betty and her family.

Betty was fascinated by my life in Iran as well as my family and was impressed that I was related to royalty. As our relationship developed, Betty encouraged me to write home more often.

I wrote to my sister Ameh and told her all about Betty. Ameh had recently moved from Korramshahr to Tehran and had told me that life was wonderful in her large and luxurious new home. I was always a little wary about writing home, and didn't do it as often as I should. The reason was that my letters always inspired Ameh to write back and, without fail, she practically demanded that I come and live with her in Iran. Although this seems like a natural thing for a sister to tell her brother, it is quite different for an Iranian man. A problem, which sits heavy in the hearts of all Iranian men who have left home for a life abroad is the extraordinary 'pull' a family exerts to draw them back under their wing. If I went back, I had this deep-rooted and seemingly irrational feeling that I wouldn't be able leave again – that they would find a way of keeping me there.

Once my internship finished, I was offered a position as an anaesthetist in the mid-size city of Corpus Christi, which sits on the southernmost tip of Texas, overlooking the Gulf of Mexico. Even in January, the temperature rarely dips below the mid-70s. Living in Corpus Christi would make quite a very pleasant change from the long dark freezing Michigan winters. Michigan State is made up of a series of vast lakes and dense forests, with not much in between. Many Americans refer to large tracts of Michigan as 'backwoods country'.

Part of the reason I wanted the job so much (apart from the $100,000 a year I was expected to earn) was because the geography in Corpus Christi reminded me of Iran. I wanted Betty to come with me but I wasn't sure if she would be prepared to move so far away from her hometown, particularly from her parents. Being a Muslim, Betty would have to convert if we were going to live together. I was pretty nervous about bringing it up, but Betty had been the first woman to tell me she loved me, so I hoped that her love knew no bounds.

One day, in the summer of 1977, Betty and I were walking in the woods near her home. We'd been strolling silently for a few minutes, lost in our thoughts and each other's company when Betty broke the silence. "You're so good to Joe and John," She said, "I want you to have your own child."

I stopped, stunned. I'd always wanted children but had let that dream go some time ago. I was getting too old, I was never going to meet anyone who would marry me, or so I'd thought.

"If we were to do that," I said, "You would have to become a Muslim."

"We've never been to church much in my family," she said, "There's nothing to stop me converting."

Betty even suggested her sons also become Muslim. Betty's response delighted me but I said it was better to let them make their own choice once they were old enough.

"There's one other thing, however," I said. "My family. They're going to want to meet you and we would have to go to Iran for that. It doesn't have to be now but at some point in the future-"

"Honey, I love you so much,' Betty replied. "I'm ready to be beside you any place on the planet."

That was all the persuading I needed. We hadn't had an argument in all the time we'd been seeing each other. Would I ever meet another woman so intent on making me happy?

I asked Betty whether she would consider living with me and moving to Corpus Christi.

She paused and then took the words right out of my mouth. "Yes! Let's get married!"

"You are the loveliest woman in the world and I think that's a very good idea!" I replied.

Betty converted to Islam in a Houston Mosque. The local Imam, an Egyptian psychologist by the name of Dr. Elmilady, was a friend of mine and he took us through the ceremony. Betty had to recite some passages from the Koran that make declare that Allah is the only god and Mohammed is his prophet, "Asyhadu anla ilaha illa Allah, wa asyhadu anna Muhammadan Rasulullah." Forty minutes later we signed a huge certificate, the physical and legal proof of Betty's conversion and left the mosque as a Muslim couple.

We married in a short simple ceremony carried out in Farsi and English, just the two of us, and we were ready to begin our lives as Dr and Mrs Mahmoody.

Before we moved in together however, Betty sent John and Joe to live with their father and despatched Lynn and Lori, to a 'distant aunt'.

She casually told me that part of the reason she had taken Lynn and Lori on was to increase her benefit payments. "But Betty," I replied, shocked. "I lost my parents; it was devastating, you shouldn't do this to the kids."

To my shame, I didn't push Betty hard enough to change her mind; John and Joe were proving to be a real handful. Secretly I was relieved not to have them around anymore and I assumed they'd be better off with their father, who – so I thought - would be able to control their wild behaviour.

It also meant I was able to devote all my energy to my beautiful wife. I surprised Betty with gifts whenever I could and tried to be as romantic as possible, posting her love notes. We spent that Christmas and New Year in our beautiful new home at No.3 Boca Raton Drive. I was in paradise. The Texan sun shone through the big, plate glass windows and filled our house with light. We looked out onto a large garden bordered by trees. This was a real step up from Michigan.

The sea front was crammed with hotels, restaurants and busy night-spots. Our house was set back a few blocks from the beach, which meant it was quieter. The exclusive Corpus Christi Country Club was just across the road and - like all the other people in our street - we became members. The club boasted a magnificent swimming pool, a golf range, an Olympic standard gymnasium and a top class restaurant. Our home was also close to the Country Club Park, a wide expanse of beautifully manicured gardens and palm trees where we'd go for a short jog each morning before I went to work.

Betty embraced the role of housewife and became active locally; together we founded the Islamic Society of South Texas (it's still going today). Whilst I was away at the hospital, Betty often popped across the road to the Country Club for fruit cocktails, where she soon made friends. Our neighbour, Margaret Barton, and Betty became inseparable. Margaret and her husband Leon were Christians and each Sunday morning they would head off to church. At the same time, Betty and I would meet with our friends from the

Islamic Society. In the afternoon we'd meet up with the Bartons again for a barbecue in the back yard.

Betty was the perfect hostess; we were always having people over. One memorable moment occurred when Akram Khanom Hakim - one of my many cousins - came for dinner with his wife.

When Betty exclaimed at the beautiful diamond ring that Akram's wife was wearing, she insisted that Betty have it. With barely a moment's hesitation she took it off her finger and placed it on Betty's and said, in true tarof and gholov style: "It's nothing, this is normal in Iran." Open-mouthed in amazement, Betty accepted the generous gift.

Betty was my miracle. It seemed to me that through Islam Betty had been presented with a set of rules and values by which to live, something that had been lacking in her own life. I was glad we were now 1,600 miles away from Betty's parents and I think Betty was too. She was really undergoing a metamorphosis in Corpus Christi.

To me, Betty's parents were crass and uneducated and although I always showed them the utmost respect, I found it hard to relate to them. Harold Lover was in his late-fifties, but he looked a lot older. He'd lost his teeth and wore dentures, as did his wife, Fern. He also had a heart condition, which I put down in part to his poor diet. Harold would eat meat and potatoes for every meal: strictly no herbs, spices or sauces and definitely no fruit or vegetables.

Harold had a temper, and had once thrown a plate, fully loaded with meat and potatoes at Fern for no good reason. I attended to Fern's cuts as she sobbed, while Betty cleaned up and Harold watched the TV, sucking on a beer.

I wasn't overly excited at the prospect of travelling back to Michigan to visit Betty's parents that first scorching summer but I couldn't put it off any longer. Shirley, Betty's sister, was getting married.

We arrived the day before and on the morning of the wedding I met Lyn and Lori in the hotel lounge with John and Joe. Betty was still upstairs applying the finishing touches to her expensive outfit. She was really looking forward to wowing the family.

"So how are things with your aunt?" I asked pleasantly.

"Awful," Lori said, "We hate her, and hate livin' with her."

"Yeah, she barely feeds us," Lyn added, "She don't care what we do or where we are as long as it don't cost her time or money."

"At least she don't beat you up," John said.

"What on earth do you mean?" I asked.

"Our dad beats us," Joe said, "It's awful, we hate him."

"Ma always said he would change but he never did," John added. "He was just like this with her. He used to beat her too."

I felt awful. I'd selfishly let these boys go home to live with their abusive father. But why had Betty decided to send them back when she herself had experienced beatings at the hands of this man?"

I couldn't understand it. It made no sense to me. I immediately started to return to our room to find Betty but ran into her in lobby.

"Hey Moody," she said casually, "have you seen the boys yet?"

"Yes I have!" I replied barely able to contain my anger, "We must go back to our room to talk about this!"

Betty frowned at me. "Calm down Moody, what's all this about?"

I know I should have waited until we were alone but I couldn't help myself.

"Joe and John are being beaten by their father. What were you thinking sending them to live with him? It's a disgrace!"

To my amazement Betty started to cry. Then she started to tremble, howl and drool before having convulsions right in front of me. She shook her body wildly, as if she were having a seizure.

I, along with the other guests in the lobby stared at her in amazement. I couldn't believe what I was seeing. I carried Betty into a side office and laid her down on a table where I started to massage her to try and ease the muscle spasms. The staff wanted to call for an ambulance but I told them I was a doctor and that it would be okay.

It took about half an hour but eventually the spasms subsided and Betty came round. This was more than enough to persuade me to let the subject rest – for the moment at least.

On the day of the wedding I was shocked when I turned to see the bride come down the aisle – Shirley was still in high school and was six months pregnant by the classmate she was about to marry.

Despite this obvious warning sign, during the reception Betty told Lyn and Lori that she wouldn't have them back and that they should move in with their boyfriends. I was astounded; the same patterns were repeating themselves from one generation of Betty's family to the next. She agreed that Joe and John would move back in, however.

Over the following weeks, Betty started to change. She cried whenever I asked her to do anything, no matter how trivial or simple, something like "We're almost out of cereal," or "I'm out of socks, could you do a wash tomorrow?"

One day, with tears in her eyes, Betty said: "You can beat me up if you want."

"What's all this?" I asked softly. "I would never hit you. You know that don't you?"

After a while, as we talked Betty began to open up about her marriage.

"He beat me for the slightest thing – and then a few hours later he'd make up with me."

It was as if she expected the same from me. Hurting her was the last thing I would ever do; all my religious beliefs, my upbringing and medical training had made me a man of peace. I cursed myself for not piecing this together much sooner. I resolved to do everything I could to make sure she would get over this and that our marriage would be stronger as a result.

A few weeks later, Betty's parents, Harold and Fern came to visit us. As Harold shook my hand, he said, "Thank you so much Moody; real swell what you've done for us!" I had no idea what he was talking about. Fern, who was just as portly as her husband, grabbed me in a rib-cracking hug, almost lifting me off the floor. "It's not everyday your son-in-law solves all your problems!" I looked at Betty, a 'what-on-earth' expression writ large across my face.

That night, when I asked her what was going on, Betty fell into another fit; when she came round she told me our savings were gone. She had paid off her parents' mortgage - without asking me first. I would have agreed to help if she had discussed it with me – apparently Harold was struggling to make the payments.

My medical practice was booming, turning over $30,000 a month. I had encouraged Betty to run the financial side of the business so I could concentrate on medicine. Betty did so - collecting expense receipts, issuing invoices and banking funds - along with the household chores, perfectly. I couldn't ask for a better business partner. We lived comfortably and within a year we'd amassed $200,000 in savings. I was confident that we would soon save the money again and I was happy that Betty was no longer worried about her parents' financial problems. But I resolved to keep a closer watch on our money, just in case Betty did something else without consulting me first.

Life continued in our large house on Boca Raton Drive. Betty cooked beautiful Iranian specialities; we held parties for friends and neighbours and Betty was a wonderful mother to her two boys once they'd moved back in. We hired a housemaid so Betty could spend more time with them.

Our first wedding anniversary in 1978 was very romantic; we hired a babysitter for Joe and John and dined at the Petroleum Club, an exclusive restaurant, while an orchestra played. When the music stopped the conductor announced 'Dr. and Mrs. Mahmoody are celebrating their first wedding anniversary,' - the other diners applauded us. I beamed, embarrassed but delighted. For the first time, it felt like my life really meant something, as if I really belonged.

That night, we came home to news reports from Iran of riots and massacres. A revolution was underway. I watched fascinated and wondered whether the impossible might happen – whether the Shah would be swept from his throne. I called home to check that everyone was okay.

After a bit of encouragement from me, Betty asked Lyn and Lori to move back in with us. But while she was happy for me to buy presents for Joe and John, she wouldn't let me get anything for the girls.

One day I came home and heard screaming as I approached the front door. My heart pounding, I dashed into the front room to find Betty yelling at Joe to 'teach Lori a lesson'. Lori had just told Betty she was pregnant by her teenage boyfriend. My appearance seemed to calm things down. Although this in itself was pretty hard for me to understand, what came next was simply unbelievable.

A few days later I was at work when Dr Elmilady's wife Saidah called me; she had become close friends with Betty. "Moody, you have to go home," she urged me, "Betty called me, she told me you've beaten her, she says she's taken all your savings and run away!"

CHAPTER EIGHT
A DIFFERENT WORLD

The female *pasdar*, clad head to foot in black screeched at Betty. The shop-keeper, with whom I had been in the midst of polite negotiation, gave a tired 'Oh no, not again,' kind of groan as I ran off to help, hugging Mahtob close. The *pasdar* had cost him a sale.

'What is it? What is it?' I asked in Farsi as I arrived beside Betty putting my arm around her trembling shoulder.

'She is not dressed appropriately!'

I looked at Betty and could see nothing out of place.

'That clip!' the *pasdar* said, climbing out of the four-by-four and marching towards us.

Betty had used a clip to hold her hair back and it had slipped forward so that it protruded from beneath her headscarf with a lock of hair. I put Mahtob down reluctantly – she was already upset at the *pasdar* shouting at her mum and I knew tears would soon follow. The *pasdar* looked as if she were going to make a grab for Betty's headscarf, as if to snatch it away but I quickly stepped in her way, turned and pushed the offending clip back into Betty's scarf with fumbling hands.

'There!' I said loudly, trying to control my outrage. 'Is that better?'

The *pasdar* glared at Betty and I through screwed-up, mean-spirited eyes before turning and walking away.

I pulled Betty close, Mahtob had grabbed my leg; Betty was close to tears and nearly crushed me in her shaking arms.

I told her that this was not so much a threat as a jealous woman trying to show her superiority. It is not really the way things are. 'That's the type of person that signs up to do these sorts of jobs,' I said.

'I'm scared Moody,' Betty replied quietly, out of Mahtob's earshot.

They day had grown hot and despite all the tea I was thirsty, shaken and needed a rest. I imagined Betty and Mahtob felt the same way.

'Come on,' I said, 'it's been a long morning, let's go home.'

'Home?' Betty said, pushing me back. 'What do you mean home? This isn't home! And it never will be!'

'Calm down,' I said, 'It's just an expression, I just meant back to my sister's house.'

I hailed a cab and soon we were fighting our way through the blaring traffic. As I sat there I wondered for a moment again whether I'd done the right thing by bringing us here.

Contradictions and double standards were part of our every aspect of our social and political life. Our bountiful supply of oil meant that we were supposed to be a wealthy nation but - thanks in no small part to the war - the country's economy was in shambles and the huge gulf between rich and poor had widened even further in recent years.

While repression was on the streets, the private walled gardens of Tehran were free. This is part of Iranian *haq*, and although the *pasdaran* patrolled the streets with a real ferocity of purpose since the revolution, homes were only very rarely invaded – only during the Shah's time and in the crazed early days of the revolution. Once they were behind the walls of their home and garden, Iranians had no fear of expressing their opinions, no matter how radical, left or right wing they might be.

Then there was the fact that many Iranians – especially those who had never left the country – didn't like America, but at the same time we were the most pro-American country in the Middle East. I'm sure that more American films and books (outlawed by the state) were (and still are) sold illegally on the black market here than anywhere else in the world.

Most worryingly, although I didn't yet realise it – although it wasn't long before I was fully appraised thanks to the newspaper reports (no attempt was made to hide the outrages) - dozens of Iranians, even children under the age of eighteen, were being executed every month by the government that professed to love its people and talked incessantly of freedom.

One of the biggest Iranian contrasts was – and still remains- the treatment of women. Historically, Iranian women have lived in a progressive society and enjoyed more equality and freedom than their Middle Eastern neighbours.

For many years women had been able to sit in Parliament, to drive, to vote, to buy property and to work. Archaeological evidence from pre-Islamic Iran suggests that ordinary women worked, sold and rented property and paid taxes. They managed large building projects and held senior military positions.

The Prophet Muhammad was the first to specifically address women's rights and recognized that men and women had different, rather than unequal, rights and responsibilities. Men were expected to provide financially, therefore women were not seen as needing legal rights, as men were there to protect and maintain them.

In reality, the arrival of Islam after the Arab conquest led to a decline in women's position at every level. Most of their rights evaporated and the Islamic dress code was imposed, polygamy was practiced and family laws were made exclusively to the advantage of the male.

Rezah Shah started legislating for women when in 1931, women were granted the right to divorce and the marriage age was raised to fifteen. By 1936, a system of education was implemented so that boys and girls were educated equally. In the same year, legislation was passed to abolish the veil, a highly controversial move. Oppression can work both ways of course. Back then, the vast majority of women in Iran could not imagine leaving the house without a chador. Suddenly, if they did wear a chador in public, it was forcibly removed, and they were sometimes beaten if they resisted.

The Shah also encouraged women to work outside the home. Women were given the vote in 1962 and six years later the family protection law, the most repressive family law in the Middle East, was ratified. Divorce laws became stringent and polygamy was discouraged. The marriage age was raised to eighteen.

Many Iranian women were active in the revolution that overthrew the Shah but I think it's safe to say that few foresaw how the adoption of a version of Sharia law and the creation of an Islamic Republic would affect their rights.

Within a couple of years of the revolution women were back in hijabs - and this time it was compulsory. The legal age of marriage plummeted to nine for girls and fifteen for boys, and society was strictly segregated. Women were not allowed to appear in public with a man who was not a husband or a direct relation, and they could be flogged for being dressed incorrectly – just for showing a few strands of hair or scraps of make-up.

Betty found Iranian dress quite hard to get used to and sometimes forgot to cover herself before leaving the house. I'd catch her by the door checking she had her purse and various make-up bits and pieces, but still thinking there was something else she'd forgotten before I reminded her. She was once half way down the road before she realized all the curious stares from passers by were because she'd left without covering her hair. If the *Pasdaran* had passed then they would have had no hesitation in arresting her.

I'm sure a great number of women would have preferred to leave the house bare-headed - as many do today - if they'd had a choice. But we were in the midst of a war and wars have the effect of making people tolerate many difficulties and although having to cover the head was a symbol of their broader lack of rights, it was not then considered the time to strike out for equality. The nation was holding on for victory.

The regime had capitalized on the war and the many people who despaired at the censorship and the ruthless elimination of the opposition kept their opinions to themselves – it wasn't yet time to speak out. We needed to win the war against Iraq, the aggressor that had invaded our country, only then we would be able to deal with all of our other problems. Sadly, the regime knew this and refused offers of cease-fires and peace talks. But even the regime realized - as the nation's blood continued to drain away into Iraq – that eventually the people of Iran would be able to stand no more.

Under the revolutionary regime, women were even restricted in their right to travel, which was not possible without a husband or father's permission. Women were completely under the control of the patriarchy. Family law fell under the jurisdiction of the religious courts and it became almost impossible for a woman to divorce her husband without his agreement, and in any case of divorce she was almost certain to lose custody of her children.

Worst of all, women were sometimes stoned to death for adultery in remoter parts of Iran, a punishment introduced by the Ayatollahs in 1979. Tragically, if a woman kills a man who has raped her, then she can be sentenced to death. But if she lets him rape her then she can be sentenced to death for adultery. A most terrible Iranian paradox.

In the years after the Revolution, women holding high positions lost their jobs and many gave up promising careers. However, women did not disappear behind a curtain this time. They had tasted emancipation and they resisted a total return to the home, leading to many more peculiarly Iranian contrasts. They held onto the rights to vote and to own property as well as to maintain financial independence after marriage. Women continued to insist on being educated, something the regime was unable to resist, especially as so many educated young men were being slaughtered in the border wars with Iraq. Women made up about two thirds of all university students, though their subsequent employment rate remained well below twenty per cent.

The experience in the market was a rude introduction for Betty, Mahtob and I into life for women in Iran. My thoughts about this were soon interrupted as we drove back to Ameh's house. While Iranians might be the most courteous people in the world, as soon as they get behind a steering wheel, they became insane monsters who would cut-up their own mother. We implored our kamikaze taxi driver to slow down – Betty's nerves were already fraught and I worried about a possible nervous breakdown.

I am sure that any foreigner who has ever visited Iran would gladly agree with me when I say that the traffic here is clearly the worst in the world. This is not because of the sheer numbers of cars and lorries on the road – it is purely down to the insanity and aggressiveness of our drivers.

And this is yet another contrast, for these are the people who would engage in the politest possible tarof with you if you met them face-to-face. And that's the reason why. Driving allows Iranians to escape tarof, for, as long as they don't make eye contact, then anything goes. The trick when crossing roads in Tehran is to make eye-contact with the driver – only then might they feel compelled to screech to a halt, smile and politely wave you across the road.

Although Tehran was six hundred miles from the fighting, it could still be a dangerous place. Not long after we arrived a massive bomb exploded near Tehran's central station during the morning rush hour, leaving the whole street a blackened shambles: burning cars, shattered windows, women in black *chadors* weeping as the wounded were carried away. Eighteen dead, three hundred wounded. This was the work of a home-grown Iranian terror group that called itself, amongst other titles, the National Liberation Army. They were determined to overthrow the Imam and so had thrown in their lot with Iraq shortly after the war started.

After the first few awkward days and weeks of adjusting to some of the stranger and more difficult differences between our two worlds, Mahtob appeared to adapt to Iranian life quite well. Although neither Betty nor I were fans of the Iranian style of dress for women, Mahtob had no problems adjusting. We always performed a systems check much like the pilots of the Apollo spacecraft before the three of us left the house and turned it into a game, so Mahtob checked that both her and Betty were properly covered. Ankles covered – check. Wrists covered – check. Hair covered – check. Okay, we're ready for lift-off!

Betty, on the other hand, was finding quite difficult. It didn't help that while Betty understandably struggled with Farsi, Mahtob picked up the new language really quickly and so was able to communicate more easily with the entire family – a vital part of moving to any country. Overall, our wonderful daughter proved how well adjusted she was by barely noticing the difference between Iran and home. In many ways, it was easier for a child as mistakes were forgiven – not that there were many to be made for children who are generally expected to be obedient no matter where they are in the world. It wasn't long before Mahtob asked if she could start school so she could meet new friends.

It was much harder for Betty and she found the cultural differences confusing and sometimes frightening. The fact that Farsi didn't come easy to her meant that she didn't know what was being said around her unless someone translated. I always interpreted for her when I was there but it's very difficult to join in with a typical fast-moving conversation this way.

When the family argued Betty started to think we were discussing her when it was something else entirely, from the price of fruit, where to get the best clothes, what was wrong with our government and the latest strategy in the war with Iraq.

The fact that Mahtob was soon able to join in with many conversations and was dearly loved by my family made Betty jealous. Mahtob's learning of

Farsi had also made us even closer and I think Betty started to resent this. Perhaps she began to feel that not only was she an outsider, but she was also losing her precious daughter to her in-laws.

On top of this were the complications of war. Normal life had all but come to a full stop. People didn't like to spend their evenings outside in case there was a bombing raid and many restaurants and cinemas shut down as a result. Civil servants were sent home early and were advised to stay indoors. The normally insanely busy streets became eerily free of traffic as nightfall approached. Until air raid sirens became the norm, we carried transistor radios with us as these proved to be the best warnings we had if a bombing raid was due.

Most inconveniently, shops started to run low on basic goods like flour, sugar and soap and prices went through the roof. Just before we arrived the government introduced rationing. To our horror, we found that the queues literally went around the block; just getting a bag of sugar meant waiting in line for up to two hours.

Once again, Betty had been thrown into the deep end. Before the war, you could just stroll to any corner where there would be an abundance of goods and your shopping bags would have been loaded within minutes.

As time went on and war became steadily more familiar, so life continued. Restaurants gradually re-opened in the evenings and people took to the streets again, enjoying tea and strolls through the city, to see friends. Tehran was still the same – albeit poorer.

Things improved somewhat when we moved in with English-speaking and America-loving Mohammed Ali (my nephew who had briefly stayed with us in America); he had two young children around Mahtob's age and spoke excellent English. Betty was pleased at the move, even though she and Mohammed Ali hadn't got on that well in the USA. She now seemed determined to make amends however, and we soon settled in.

I'd wasted no time in getting my paperwork in order so I could start treating the victims of war as soon as possible and while I waited for the bureaucratic clogs of the Islamic revolution to turn, Betty, Mahtob, Mohammed and I 'did' Tehran and beyond - from the base of the snow-capped Mount Damavand, which towers 19,000 feet to the north of the city, to the holiest sites of Shiite Islam, including the shrines in the cities of Qom, Masshad and Isfahan.

When we did visit one of the Shah's palaces it was, I had to admit, a bit of a disappointment. Stripped bare of all its opulent furnishings, we wondered through its bare corridors as the guide told us about the unconscionable view the Shah had of all the poor living in view if his windows.

Much better was a trip to Park Mellat, two weeks after we arrived, arranged at the suggestion of Majit. As Zia's successful business partner in the manufacture of cosmetics, Majit seemed to have plenty of leisure time and a sense of humour to boot. Betty was right to call him the 'joker' and Mahtob screamed with delight as they played.

It was a beautiful day and at the end of it, I felt as if we really could be happy here.

Sadly, the State had other ideas.

CHAPTER NINE
ON THE RUN

I dropped the phone and ran through the hospital corridors to my car; I was in shock. Surely Betty must have known Saidah - whom Betty counted as a close friend - would have called me.

My mind raced as I fought my way home through the traffic. Was I that bad a husband? Betty had seemingly borne my faults without question. I wasn't perfect, not by a long stretch; I could sometimes live up to my nickname 'Moody' and lapse into silence for no good reason. I was shy and awkward socially and often felt as though I was embarrassing Betty in front of our friends.

My hands shook as I fumbled for the house keys. To my relief, Betty was still there, in our bedroom, throwing clothes into a suitcase half-filled with cash. As soon as she saw me she flipped, tearing at her hair and beating her fists on the floor.

"Don't worry," I said, "it's okay, I forgive you; it's alright. It's alright."

I marched up to Betty, got down on the floor next to her and held her tightly until she stopped shaking.

"I didn't want to do it," she told me.

"I know, my love" I said, "We'll never mention this again, if you don't want to."

My heart ached physically at the sight of Betty so helpless; even though I was a doctor, I didn't know what I could do to stop it and I hated this feeling of powerlessness. But whatever it would take, we would stay together. Betty was my lover and my best friend, just being together in bed was indescribably wonderful; I loved waking up with her in the mornings.

Betty and I really needed to speak to a psychologist. Back in the 1970's psychology and counselling was nothing like it is today and no one talked about these sorts of problems.

I tried to work it out for myself. Why had Betty tried to take our savings and run away, and why had she then given the game away by calling Saidah?

I wondered if her behaviour had something to do with her lifelong poverty. While we were still in Michigan, I often brought the kids parcels of food and other goodies that Betty couldn't afford, just simple things, like Hershey's Chocolates, real coffee or expensive ice cream. I didn't know whether her former husband paid any alimony but it certainly didn't look like it. She found all sorts of ways to save and make little bits of money, but nonetheless relied on the support of the charitable group Friends of the Court to provide money for food and bills.

I'd never had to worry about how to pay the electricity bill, where the next month's groceries would come from or how to feed the kids. These were everyday concerns for Betty. Betty worked all the hours she could at a tough job in a factory. She was a survivor.

I imagined that the stresses of her impoverished life had caused her breakdowns, including the one she'd suffered when we first met.

Perhaps her sudden change from her life as a single mum in Michigan into a doctor's wife in an affluent suburb of Corpus Christi, 1,600miles from her home-town had been too sudden, almost psychologically traumatising in fact. Had Betty had a panic attack that had switched her back into her 'former' self, a self where she needed to seize every opportunity to survive?

It was obvious to me that Betty didn't want to talk about it and I could appreciate that. Things between us were back to normal the next day and I was soon distracted by international events as Iran spent more and more time in the news headlines.

The dictatorial, CIA-installed, Western-friendly regime headed by the Shah was on the verge of collapse. The Shah had modernised Iran but his dreaded secret police ruthlessly crushed any opposition.

Now, in the name of the exiled Ayatollah Khomeini, Islamic revolutionaries tried to topple the royal regime. In January 1979, the Shah fled Iran and on February 1 the Ayatollah Khomeini arrived in Iran as guerrillas defeated the Shah's troops on the streets of Tehran. By April, Iran had been totally transformed; it was a unique event, the twentieth century's first popular religious revolution; its speed and success shocked the world.

Religious men had somehow instated a mediaeval system of government on a rich country with a modern economy and a large, well-educated middle-class. Even though they were aristocratic, my family were strict Shiites and welcomed the change.

Betty was right when she told me that the revolution had little meaning for us in the US, thousands of miles away – but that would change soon enough.

CHAPTER TEN
BREAKDOWNS

Despite being desperate for doctors, the Health Ministry delayed my application, offering no explanation apart from the occasional convoluted, near-indecipherable letter.

While I was embroiled in my bureaucratic chase, the $10,000 in cash I had brought with us was shrinking fast, even though it was worth six times as much on the black market.

I normally collected Mahtob from school after my daily trip to the Ministry but one day, to my surprise, I found Betty already there. "What's wrong?" I asked her, thinking that something bad might have happened.

"Mahtob's been crying," Betty said, "the principal called me. I'm going to take Mahtob to and from school each day from now on."

I knelt down next to Mahtob, gently held her shoulders. "What're you afraid of, darling?" I asked.

"I'm afraid of being taken away from mummy," Mahtob replied. "I want her to wait there for me every day."

"No one's going to take you away. What is it that you're afraid of?" I asked.

Suddenly Betty turned on me and said: "Why don't you just leave her alone!" I didn't want to argue in front of Mahtob, so left it at that.

Betty's behaviour changed from that day: "Iranians are a smelly, dirty bunch of liars," she said, and she told Mahtob there were cockroach wings in the soup. The 'wings' were nothing more than fried tomato skins, but it was enough to kill Mahtob's appetite.

While Iran was of course drastically different from America, it was not as bad as Betty seemed to think. She now simply refused to learn any Persian, which only reinforced her perceived isolation and increased her distorted view

– a view she now seemed determined to push onto Mahtob, who only grew confused by the difference between Betty's words and what she experienced.

As Betty's aggressive and resentful attitude continued, the patience of some of my family and friends started to wear thin. Majid told me to do something but as to what, well, I simply didn't know.

Betty was under huge pressure to conform and behave in the correct manner, something she wasn't used to doing – 'behaving correctly' in the States just meant being normal and required little effort and even when the rules were broken the consequences were usually minor. In Iran, public displays of disobedience could lead to imprisonment if the police became involved. Cultural ignorance would never be accepted as an excuse.

Once again, I should have spoken to Betty about the pressure-cooker situation she was now in. I still hadn't learned my lesson from our previous experiences and like Betty I was caught between two worlds. I had a sense that things were starting to unravel and that another breakdown was on the cards, but I did all I could to push those thoughts away.

I was here to do important work, to help my fellow countrymen. I had long glorified my dead parents as selfless individuals who had sacrificed their lives to ease the suffering of others and I aspired to be just like them.

To that end, I made almost daily trips to the Ministry of Health to hurry along the paperwork. Meanwhile, Betty kept Mahtob away from my family as much as possible so that she would not become more tied to her Iranian side.

Betty stopped trying to be a part of the household and spent most of her time when I was away in her room with Mahtob and scowled whenever my sister knocked on the door and tried to persuade them to come with her to the market, to visit someone, to go sightseeing and so on. I understand why she did this now but at the time I just found it infuriating.

A solution presented itself in the run up to Mahtob's fifth birthday party. Surely Betty would want to be involved in the organisation of that? When I brought it up, Betty immediately wanted to change the date of the party to midweek, as opposed to the weekend. 'But everybody's off work at the weekend,' I said. 'If we have it midweek then some people won't be able to come. And it's a school night.'

But Betty was adamant: 'I want to have it on her birthday.'

Sensing a tantrum, I quickly gave in and we went shopping for a doll for Mahtob. Betty picked up an ugly looking foreign thing, the most expensive doll we'd seen and demanded I get it for Mahtob. Sensing that Betty was still on the edge and not wishing to argue (I wasn't sure that Mahtob would actually like it), I agreed.

Both of us had spent most of our marriage avoiding confrontation – only talking about our problems when we were on the verge of disaster or in the midst of a crisis. Coming to Iran had most certainly put us in both of those categories. Although I knew the problems were there and could see they were getting worse I didn't want to face them.

Shortly before Mahtob's birthday, Betty and I went to collect a huge cake from a bakery near our home. It was a cheerful bright yellow and as long as my arm – but hadn't been decorated.

Recalling happier times, when Betty iced my birthday cake in Farsi, I suggested she do the same with Mahtob's. This, I imagined, would go down very well with my family. I was so pleased with the idea that I told the baker what a fantastic cake decorator she was.

'Perhaps she would like to come and work here!' the baker joked in English.

Betty was not amused. She simply shook her head and said no.

The party was enormous affair, more the size and scale of a wedding with a hundred guests, many of whom had taken the time off work. Ameh worked in the kitchen all day preparing a feast of Iranian dishes while her daughters decorated the table with vegetables that they'd carved into a surprising number of shapes, including carrots cut to resemble tulips laid out on beds of bright green herbs. Bunches of tiny Persian limes were hung on the doors. The air was cool and the room smelled wonderful.

There's nothing quite like the laughter of children to put a smile on the face of adults and a joyous mood filled the house. After much singing, eating and the playing of games, the time finally arrived for the 'grand opening'. Mahtob had amassed a huge pile of brightly wrapped presents that towered over her as she stared at them in wonder. Once she had unwrapped them – clothes, dolls, balls and toys for the swimming pool - and thanked everyone, the children started to play together again. As they did so, and as Mahtob talked more and more in Farsi, Betty became more and more withdrawn and tried to make Mahtob sit with her, away from the rest of the party. Of course, she was never going to manage this with the guest of honour and Betty simply became moodier as the day went on, although she stood by Mahtob as she blew out the candles on her birthday cake. She was also there as Mahtob climbed onto the red bicycle Betty and I had chosen together after we'd bought the doll. Betty couldn't help herself and smiled as I pushed Mahtob along the garden, a proud moment for all concerned. Our daughter was growing up! Mahtob talked about nothing else for days afterwards.

The war made another significant intrusion into our lives not long after the birthday party. Occasionally, although Tehran was hundreds of miles from the front line, Iraqi Scuds roared across the city sky. In a city of ten million people the chances of being hit were minute and most of the time they fell well short of Tehran.

Nonetheless, as the warnings came, Betty would scream hysterically "Oh my God, we're all gonna die!" and grabbed hold of Mahtob, nearly crushing her. Mahtob was understandably frightened but Betty's over the top reaction meant that my efforts to reassure her failed miserably.

Betty continued to drive a wedge between us. As I wondered how to deal with this, an unseen missile that had been hurtling towards me for some time suddenly exploded into our lives.

CHAPTER ELEVEN
THE LADY VANISHES

I stood dumbfounded. My heart thumped. I was the first and only customer in the bank that morning. The cashier leaned over her desk: "Your balance is zero, Mr Mahmoody," she repeated.

"When was the money withdrawn and by whom?" I asked, my hands trembling, already knowing the answer.

The cashier looked at me as if I were quite mad and said, "Why, your wife, sir, she withdrew $200,000 yesterday." I stood, stupefied for some time. "Sir?" the cashier asked me, "Sir, is everything alright?"

No, it most certainly was not.

In late January Betty said that she wanted to go and visit her parents. I was a little surprised because the weather in Michigan had been so appalling. Six feet of snow had fallen in Banister, her parents' hometown. When I turned on the TV I saw that people having to dig their cars out of snowdrifts. The roads were all but deserted.

"Why don't we wait until the snow's melted?" I asked her.

"We should go now Moody, I need to see my folks, it's been so long and I miss them so much."

I couldn't get time off work at such short notice, so Betty said she'd go on her own. Her flight was early, before my shift started, so I was able to drive her to the airport. It was early when we pulled out of our drive, but already the air was warm and balmy. As we headed out along Saratoga Boulevard on the thirty-minute drive to Corpus Christi International Airport, I asked Betty about her father. Harold wasn't exactly a picture of health and I wondered if she'd heard something or was worried about something that she wasn't sharing with me.

"He's fine, Moody," she said continuing to look out of the window. I noticed she was constantly fidgeting with her handbag and wouldn't look at me whenever I tried to start a conversation. She wasn't afraid of flying, so it wasn't that.

Once we were at the departures desk I kissed and hugged her.

"I love you," I said.

"Yeah, I love you too," Betty said quickly. "I'll call from Mom and Dad's just as soon as I arrive, to let you know everything's okay."

The hours passed and no call. I checked with the airline.

"The flight's been re-routed via Chicago," a woman told me, "the weather ain't been this bad for years, I don't know why anybody would want to travel in this."

By seven o'clock that evening I'd still not heard from Betty. Even with delays it was unlikely the journey would have taken this long. I was a bit hesitant to call her parents as Fern had a tendency to develop hysteria over the slightest thing, but I was now really worried. I needed to know why Betty hadn't rung.

As always, Harold answered the phone. Fern seemed to spend her whole time either in the kitchen, frying meat and potatoes, or glued to the TV watching soap operas. I could hear a melodrama blaring away in the background as I spoke to Harold.

"Beddy? You're after Beddy?" Harold yelled above the TV. "Ain't seen nor heard nuddin', Moody."

"Can you make sure she calls me as soon as she gets in?' I asked. 'Only, she should have been with you hours ago.'

'Sure thing, bud,' Harold replied.

I waited another hour but the phone didn't ring. I called back. Again, Harold told me that he'd not heard anything. By ten o'clock I was getting seriously worried. I phoned again.

"No Moody," Harold said testily, "I told ya I'll call as soon as Beddy gets here. Just sit tight will ya?"

Harold was obviously annoyed by my repeated calls but this didn't make sense. Why wasn't he worried? By now I was completely unnerved and images of Betty in hospital or worse, injured, trapped in a car at the side of the road in the snow kept appearing before my mind's eye. 'Please,' I thought, 'please let Betty be safe.'

I called the Michigan police department and asked if there'd been any serious air or road accidents. Nothing.

Perhaps she'd decided to go and stay with another of her relatives in Michigan. Betty certainly had plenty to choose from, as the Lover clan was a big one. Each of Harold's six children seemed to have had a similarly large number of offspring.

I called Harold again. "D'you think Betty would have gone to stay with one of her brothers or sisters?"

"Nope Moody, don't think she would. Listen, I gotta go, OK?"

I sank into the sofa and gazed out over our floodlit back lawn. I was certain that Harold did know the truth, otherwise why show no concern for Betty's safety?

Could it be that Betty was there at his house, but that Harold was trying to hide that fact from me? And if that was the case, the question then was why was Harold lying?

I finally got to bed at around one o'clock in the morning, but sleep just wouldn't come. I kept running over all the day's events in my mind. I hoped Harold had lied for that meant that Betty was alive and well. That also meant that Betty had done something wrong and wanted to hide from me. I hated myself for suspecting my wife in this way but it was unavoidable.

What next? All other flights to Michigan had been cancelled because of the bad weather; the airport told me the next flight wouldn't leave until at least midday tomorrow.

The following morning, after a few hours of nightmarish half-sleep, my mind full of suspicion, I travelled down to my bank. After the teller told me that Betty had emptied our account I just stood there, my head spinning.

Did Betty love me? Had it been a sham? Did she suffer from some psychosis or was she just after our money? Betty had told me many wonderful things; that she wanted my children, would live with me anywhere. She acted so kindly, loved me so beautifully and had converted to Islam. Had she said and done all this simply to take our money and run?

I drove home on autopilot. I felt numb. In one blow she had destroyed all that we had built. I felt heartbroken. My visions of a family life, of children, of sunny days spent with our kids in the park, were shattered.

When I'd met and married Betty I had allowed myself to imagine a life where I would never have to be alone again. Now, after what Betty had done, I could only imagine one outcome: separation and divorce. And if that did happen then perhaps I only had myself to blame. I'd been so blinded by love and the desire for all the wonderful things I imagined marrying Betty would bring. I was a fool. I knew that Betty was a good person, she just wasn't well and I had blinded myself to the possibility that her illness had resurfaced. There had been signs in the weeks leading up to her trip to Michigan.

"Fool!" I said out loud. "Well you married her now Moody and that means something. The least you can do is make the effort to save your marriage!"

By the time I arrived back home, I'd come up with a plan of action. I called Harold.

"I have a message I'd like you to give Betty. If she doesn't contact me in the next twenty-four hours, I will go to the police and tell them about her withdrawing all our money and will immediately sue for divorce. By proving her theft in court I will also deprive her of all her rights to any property. Is that clear?'

There was a second's silence.

"Yeeaah, kinda," Harold said eventually. "I'll let Beddy know. Say, Moody, don't go doin' nothin' hasty now, will ya?"

So I was right. Betty was there. I could do nothing more now, so I decided to go in to work. At least it might keep my mind off of things. My job was so important I had to concentrate and I always found that it focussed my mind no matter what else was going on.

Once I broke for lunch I had a call from Dr Moazzim Haydar, the chairman of our Islamic group.

"Moody, I need to talk to you about a delicate family matter."

My heart leapt. "Did Betty call you?"

"Yes," Dr Haydar said gently. "She's told me all that she's done, and she asks for your forgiveness."

"What did she tell you?" I asked him, half-dreading the answer.

While I was mortified that Betty hadn't felt able to call me; I was glad she had contacted me through Dr Haydar. She must have thought, mistakenly, that I'd be furious with her and by approaching Dr Haydar, she showed she still l cared for me and that she wanted to repair the damage. As my elder and a respected Muslim community leader, she knew I would respect whatever Dr Haydar had to say.

Nonetheless I was deeply embarrassed and I wondered if I could ever look Dr. Haydar in the eye again.

"Can you tell Betty to call me?" I asked him, hopefully.

"Of course," he replied. Suddenly his voice took on a joyful tone. "But Moody, there's something else. She's given me some wonderful news. You're going to be overjoyed – your wife is expecting!"

Chapter Twelve
ENEMY OF THE REVOLUTION

I stood in the reception of the Ministry of Health, fuming at a group of scruffy young officials who were refusing to tell me why my license hadn't yet materialised.

"Why don't you deal with this?" I demanded, "You want doctors, yet you're keeping me from helping!"

One of them marched up to me and shoved a finger in my face. "Tell us your REAL reason for returning to Iran!" he yelled, "Then we might help you!"

A sudden chill hit me. Things had really changed. They saw me as the enemy. I was an American-educated doctor, clean-shaven, dressed in a suit and tie. They had never left Iran, sported wild beards and wore shabby old clothes. They suspected me of spying – such Enemies of the Revolution were either executed or left to rot in the infamous Evin prison, home to hangings and torture, run by the scarred and sunken-faced sadist Azadollah Lajavardi, who was, before the revolution, a simple curtain-seller who had himself spent time in Evin for conspiring against the Shah.

Shortly after this a huge public demonstration only served to reinforce the idea that I'd made a mistake. The crowd, which was a quarter of a million strong was celebrating the first five years of the Imam's rule – and was made up of the widowed and wounded, army volunteers and veterans and thousands upon thousands of Tehran's ordinary citizens. There was no shortage of "Death to America!" slogans alongside "Death to Israel!" and "Death to France!" not forgetting "Death to Russia!"

The thirty-five-year-old Ahmed Khomeini, son of Ayatullah Ruhollah Khomeini, called for Islamic unity. Thunderous roars of approval arose as young victims of the war passed by on parade, swathed in bandages or seated in wheelchairs. Around them on every side, portraits of a glowering

Khomeini stared down on them. The city was full of patriotic fever bordering on hysteria.

This was a real wake-up call. Iran seemed to me to be simply too dangerous. We had to leave. If I ended up in jail I would lose Betty and Mahtob. They would have to go back to the US. I told Betty my doubts and finished by saying "They'll never let me practice medicine. We're going back to America."

"But you came to help the Iranians," Betty countered. "Don't give up so easy." She reminded me that after only a few of weeks at school, Mahtob was already on the way to being top of her class; it would be a pity not to let her complete a full school year. My head spun at Betty's U-turn. Could she actually be happy? Perhaps she liked this way of life? Even though she had criticised Iran time and again, she had never expressed a desire to return to the US. Strengthened by Betty's reasoning, I thought about it. We prayed together and I agreed we should stick it out.

Reassured, I resumed my daily visits to the Ministry and I grew optimistic that my persistence would finally pay off.

One day as I left the building after a particularly long and frustrating wait, Majid ran up to me, an anxious expression furrowing his normally cheerful face.

"Betty and Mahtob are missing!" he said.

"What?" I asked puzzled.

"Betty went shopping with Mahtob this morning and hasn't come back!'

I wasn't sure whether to worry or not. "Perhaps the queues were particularly bad-"

"They've been gone eight hours! Nobody knows where they are!"

I thought for a moment. Eight hours wasn't really that long. OK, it was quite a long time to spend food shopping, even with the queues. But it was possible that she might have decided to do something else with Mahtob afterwards. I tried to calm Majid and we returned home together.

Just as we arrived Betty pulled up in a taxi with Mahtob. Looking a bit sheepish, she smiled and said she'd gotten lost and that was that.

Just a few days later, after a sudden flurry of letters and forms to and from the Ministry, I got my license. I was so happy I skipped though the house singing at the top of my voice. Finally! The next day I started work at

Shohadaye Tajrish Hospital. Both of our moods improved. Betty had been right to stick it out.

The only problem was that I hardly saw Mahtob; on my days off Betty would spend hours in the bedroom and bathroom with Mahtob, and Betty nearly always sent her to bed before I came home from work.

To celebrate my new job, I ordered a new car, so we could take Mahtob on outings on our own, to see many cultural delights that lay beyond the city. While Mahtob was delighted Betty launched into a racist rant against Iranians. I asked Mahtob to go to her room.

"How dare you speak ill of Iranian culture in front of Mahtob!"

Betty screwed up her face "Iranians have no culture!" she spat, "This country is backwards."

"But our daughter is half-Iranian," I replied. "And stop separating her from me, stopping me from even being able to talk to her!"

And then Betty hit me.

Chapter Thirteen
MOONLIGHT

Wishing me a speedy reconciliation with Betty, Dr. Haydar rang off. I sat there, simultaneously stunned, overjoyed and confused – my head span. My wife was going to have a baby. But just a few minutes earlier I had been ready for divorce.

The sudden loud ring of the phone jerked me away from my thoughts. I picked up the receiver.

"*La ilaha elallah, le ilaha elallah,*" ('There is no God but God'), Betty said repeating the phrase over and over again.

She had managed to learn the basic Islamic prayer – the equivalent of The Lord's Prayer - by rote.

If she was trying to impress me with her recital it wasn't working.

"Betty, come back home," I said, cutting her off in mid-flow. "Just come home. We need to talk."

She arrived the following morning looking tired and anxious. I could see the exhaustion in the dark rings around her eyes. I made coffee and we sat facing each other over the kitchen table.

"Is it true?" I asked her. "What Dr. Haydar said about you being pregnant, is it true?"

"Yeah, it is," Betty murmured, a faint smile creeping across her face. Despite everything, my heart gave a kick of joy.

"How many months?" I asked her.

"Three," she replied and paused to consider while I sat trying to digest this. "Almost four."

"Why didn't you tell me?" I asked.

Betty didn't answer. She hung her head and stared at the floor.

I knew then that had to forgive her; more than anything I wanted us to have a child and I did not want to lose Betty – I loved her despite her extraordinary behaviour, despite the fact she had run off with our life savings when she was three months pregnant. It was a childish act, after all how could she hope to have gotten away with it? She sometimes lost control; that was all and she needed me to be there for her at those times.

"Betty, I love you and forgive you," I said. "This is wonderful news. Let's start afresh from here, OK?"

Betty nodded, but kept staring at the floor and said nothing.

"You know you don't need to pretend to be so religious with me. The most important thing in our world now is our child."

I still couldn't understand Betty's behaviour, or why she had failed to tell me she was expecting. Yet I felt I had no choice but to forgive her. The news that she was expecting a child – our child – made all things forgivable as far as I was concerned.

The next morning I went and deposited the $200,000 back in our bank account. The cashier couldn't but help give me a funny look as I did so. What Betty must have felt like travelling halfway across America and back with that amount of cash in her handbag I couldn't imagine.

When I returned home from work that evening I found an Iranian flag folded on the walnut desk in my study. I went and found Betty in the lounge.

"I've seen the flag," I said, smiling. "Where did you find it? It's such a lovely, thoughtful gift."

"I've had it a while," Betty said meekly. "I found this shop selling countries' flags n' stuff when we were on one of your conference trips."

I was touched and delighted. From then on, the months in the run-up to our daughter's birth were a time of immense joy and I felt closer to Betty than ever before. I fashioned a specially lengthened stethoscope so that Betty could listen to our baby's heartbeat.

When we went to bed I placed it on Betty's bump. I listened to our baby's heartbeat. It was so small, rapid and fragile sounding. It was like a miracle, knowing that my child was growing inside Betty's womb, knowing that in a few months' time I would be holding a little baby boy or a girl in my arms.

I felt a massive urge to do everything I could to protect and cherish our growing child. I wanted our child to grow up with both parents in a loving family and a secure home – things that had been missing from both of our childhoods. The closer we got to the time of the birth the happier and more excited I became. Our lives completely resumed their normal sunny pace at No.3, Boca Raton Drive.

On 4 September, 1979, as the Ayatollah Taleghani died and Ayatollah Kohemeni consolidated his rule, and as Iranian students rioted outside the Beverly Hills home of the Shah's sister, Betty went into labour.

When she called me at work to tell me I felt excitement rippling through me. I rushed home from work and drove Betty to the maternity hospital as fast as I safely could.

I stood by Betty's side gripping her hand as the medics administered the anaesthetic under my watchful gaze. She was given a continuous epidural, which meant that she had a painless delivery. Four hours after Betty had started her contractions our baby girl was born.

We had a healthy, lively little girl! I was truly overjoyed.

As the doctor handed me my daughter and as Betty watched, I wept and laughed; I imagined that my parents must have felt the same emotions when they held me for the first time. Suddenly I felt closer to them than ever before and distant, misty memories of my mother became a little sharper.

We were shown to a private room in the maternity ward, and mother and baby settled in for the night.

"How are you feeling my love?" I asked Betty.

"Wonderful Moody," she murmured, almost inaudibly, "just as fine as can be."

I held her hand and gazed down at our tiny little baby.

Betty, who was still quite heavily sedated, mumbled something.

The smile dropped from my face; I couldn't have heard her right. I leaned forward: "Say that again my love."

"You're not the first doctor who's given me a child."

Chapter Fourteen
FEMME FATALE

Betty leapt up with a yell and punched me in the side of my head. Betty was heavier than me and she had all her weight behind that right-hook; my glasses snapped and flew from my face as I tumbled to the floor. Before I could take a breath, Betty leapt on top of me and tore at my face with her nails.

"You have no right to say that!" She screamed. "Mahtob's not even yours!"

Her hands went to my throat. Seeing stars, choking, I fought back in desperation; bending her arms until she suddenly tumbled to the side. Betty scrambled up and ran to Mahtob's room. Still choking, I got up only to see Betty dragging a sleepy Mahtob into the room.

"Look!" she shouted, "Daddy is fighting with me!"

Mahtob, obviously confused and frightened, began sobbing.

Betty had often told me that members of her family had been abused and I'd witnessed it once with my own eyes when Harold hurled a plateful of food at Fern's head, leaving her with a deep gash.

"You dumb-dumb!" he'd yelled as blood poured over his wife's face. "I told you, I hate cold food!"

But I'd never known the women to beat the men.

After Betty calmed down, she went to the bedroom and slammed the door. I heard Mahtob crying and went to comfort her. Mahtob turned her face away from me. I hated myself for allowing this to happen, my little girl was frightened and I felt helpless; the woman I loved, the mother of our child had physically attacked me and I didn't know what to do.

Betty was subdued the following morning and so I carried on as planned, spending the day organising our move into a large, luxurious rented apartment in an exclusive district of Tehran. It had a guest suite where I planned to set up a small private medical practice for local people to run alongside my hospital work. There was an acute shortage of general practitioners in Tehran, a city that had swelled by four million people since the start of the war. Many veterans who had returned home were experiencing the after affects of the gas attacks as well as depression and excruciating phantom limb pain, a crippling neuropsychological condition. Although Tehran was well stocked with basic medicines, more sophisticated treatments, medicines and equipment that were commonplace in the USA were missing.

Once we had moved into our own home, I was hopeful that I might spend more time with Mahtob. I tried to talk to Betty again about this. But she was having none of it. All her acquiescence had vanished "You just be careful," she yelled, "And keep goddamn quiet." I tried again and Betty just turned on me, again clawing at me with her nails; again dragging a traumatized Mahtob to witness the fight.

The next day, I received a phone call from the school principal, Miss Shaheem. To my great surprise she told me she had reached the end of her tether with Betty who had abused the school's hospitality and would have to "cease coming immediately". Her daily presence was bad for Mahtob; she separated her from the other girls and Betty had spent all her time using the office telephone, running up quite a bill.

"And then, if that weren't enough, she received visitors at our office, as if it were hers!"

"What?" I asked, incredulous.

"Just the other day. A woman arrived who said she was from the US Interests Section of the Swiss Embassy."

Chapter Fifteen
HOSTAGE SITUATION

Before she passed out Betty told me that her son John had been fathered by her then doctor. She'd simply claimed he was her ex-husband's and this had been accepted. My head spun. The happiest moment of my life was somewhat blunted by this revelation.

I worried what else Betty might have kept from me, also what had made Betty entrust a child to an apparently violent man who was not the natural father. But, as I looked at my daughter, I thought this was a long time ago, a difficult time in Betty's life when she didn't have me by her side.

Betty had passed out; the room was silent. I looked out of the window and as I watched the full moon rise, my heart filled with joy and optimism. In the darkness our baby glowed under its silvery light.

Moonlight, *Mahtob* - that would be her name.

Betty wasn't keen on the name Mahtob. I'd written it on the birth certificate before Betty had a chance to put her case for a more Western sounding name. I sometimes mistakenly made decisions like this without consulting her, something she really hated – but this was something I seemed incapable of stopping. Betty's preferred first name, Miryam, became Mahtob's middle name.

. . .

In November 1979, two months to the day after Mahtob's birth, a group of student Islamic revolutionaries took over the US Embassy in Tehran and held fifty-two American diplomats hostage. I had until then expressed support for the Iranian revolution – the Shah ran a brutal regime and the revolt that overthrew and replaced him was largely peaceful, although there were rumours of many unwarranted executions.

Until the hostage crisis, nobody in the US seemed to care – before then I constantly found myself explaining where and what Iran was exactly (although after the revolution it became easier, saying it was the country where the Ayatollah overthrew the Shah was usually enough to do it).

Now, however, innocent Americans were in danger and opinion turned against me. Some colleagues branded me 'Dr Kohemeni' and, in a flash, after twenty years in America, I was suddenly the enemy.

The entire world was appalled at Iran's behaviour. Iran and Iranians now projected an image not only of scary-sounding Islamic fundamentalism and religious extremism but also of violence against Western interests. Many American Iranians said they were Persian to distance themselves from the angry mobs that screamed anti-American slogans that seemed to be on TV every night for the 444 days of the crisis. Some even changed their names to sound more American. Hussein became Harry and Mohammed became Michael and so on.

I regularly prayed for a quick and peaceful end to the crisis so that life could get back to normal. But the affair dragged on, and Betty became gripped by an irrational anger. She cursed Iran in front of our friends, trying to get me to join her. When I refused, Betty's vitriol increased; she called me a "fanatic" and "wife beater". She confided in our friends behind my back, telling them that our marriage was in trouble, which it was but I wished she'd talk to me. Whenever I tried she grew hysterical or left the house.

Unfortunately for him, my nephew Reza came to stay at this time. He had just finished university and was looking for a job. Betty goaded John and Joe against Reza and me. After a week, unable to stand it any more, my poor nephew left.

It was then that I spotted an opening for an anaesthesiologist in Michigan, near Betty's parents. Suddenly inspired, I suggested we move. Betty was overjoyed. We found a wonderful new house in Alpena, three hours' drive from Harold and Fern.

It was stunning. The enormous garden ran down to the banks of the idyllic Alpena Creek, which was part of a nature reserve. I bought a small boat and cruised the quiet waters with little Mahtob at my side.

Harold loved fishing and joined us several times; one day he landed a massive carp. "Gee. I ain't never seen such a great goddamn fish!" I had it stuffed as a surprise birthday present, "The best I ever had," he told me. Even John and Joe's behaviour improved. When sixteen-year-old Joe complained to us that his dad wouldn't teach him to drive, Betty and I taught him using our car. He passed his test first time and we bought him a second-hand car as a reward.

Rejuvenated by our move, I did all I could for Betty's family. I purchased a chainsaw for Betty's out-of-work brother, seeds and farm tools for Betty's sister, Carolyn, who was struggling to support her six children.

But the Iraqi invasion of Iran on 22 September 1980 changed everything. Saddam Hussein's air force dropped mustard gas in an attempt to win a quick victory and claim a section of oil rich land for Iraq. Iranian volunteers flocked to the battlefront and somehow managed to hold the Iraqi army off in desperate, suicidal fighting.

It was brutal right from the get-go. Tens of thousands of young volunteers known as Basij - many of whom were under ten-years-old – were shipped out to the front on buses where they were presented with miniature portraits of the Imam as well as the keys to heaven – plastic keys which they hung round their necks. In a sign that they knew absolutely what was expected of them, some brought their own funeral shrouds in their backpacks. On the morning before 'battle' they were treated to the spectacle of an actor riding a white charger, telling them war stories from Iranian legend such as the Battle of Karbala and extolling the glory of martyrdom.

Then they were sent out in wave after wave, either to clear minefields for more experienced soldiers or to be simply cut down by machine guns and mortars. Oddly enough, although many thousands were shot down by enemy fire, every now and then, a unit of Iraqi soldiers, perhaps stunned and too appalled to shoot unarmed children, deserted their positions, handing short-lived victories to the surprised suicide squads who had fully expected to be opening the gates to heaven, not standing alive and well in Iraqi bankers.

In the US, Betty and her family sided with Iraq against me. Joe and John were particularly vitriolic and I'm sure they had no idea just quite how much their comments hurt. We'd had our tough times together but I'd loved them dearly; I'd carried them on my shoulders when they were younger and cheered them through sports days like any father would. I found it unbearable they should attack me in this way. I had spent more time in the US than Iran; I adored the country that gave me my family and our livelihood.

A few days after war broke out, a rare moment of peace and quiet in our household was suddenly shattered by Mahtob's screams which tore through the house; I was up and running before I was awake. "I'm coming, I'm coming!"

When I saw her my stomach flipped. My two-year-old baby was lying on the floor, her arm wrenched out at an ungodly angle, bone pushing against skin. John was standing nearby; he had swung Mahtob around so hard he'd dislocated her shoulder.

"Idiot!" I yelled. "What have you done?"

Mahtob could suffer permanent damage if it wasn't fixed quickly. Grimacing, I gripped her shoulder; feeling the socket I gave it a sharp twist and the bone snapped back into place with a sickening "CRACK".

I scooped Mahtob up into my arms and held her close as her screams softened with the gradual easing of the terrible pain.

It was snowing heavily and Betty, not having seen the dislocation and not immediately realising the possible consequences of such a traumatic injury, didn't want to take Mahtob to hospital.

Without wanting to prolong the discussion, I wrapped Mahtob in a blanket and drove to the ER as quickly as I dared on the icy roads. She needed X-Rays and to be seen by a specialist to make sure she was okay.

Mahtob had nightmares afterwards, waking us several times. It was pretty trying but I was shocked when Betty snapped. "You're driving me crazy!" she yelled. "I wish I had gone ahead and got rid of you!"

Furious, I asked her what she meant but Betty buried her head under her pillow and refused to answer. Knowing that pressing her would lead to a 'fit', I stupidly and cowardly let the subject drop.

Had Betty's attempt to run away been part of a plan to steal our savings and abort our child? It was only after I caught her that she told me she was pregnant – an attempt to soften my anger, to prevent me from involving the police. No, it was inconceivable. Betty clearly adored Mahtob and had loved every moment of her pregnancy. It was simply a mania that sometimes took her emotions out of her control, and she said hurtful things in the heat of the moment - I just couldn't keep up.

I felt trapped, at a loss. Betty and her family turned more and more against me. I don't think anyone can truly understand what it is like to be in an abusive relationship until you have lived it and I would not wish it on my worst enemy.

I had occasionally seen cases of abuse at the hospital and I never understood why people put up with it. Now I understand that no matter how educated, intelligent and emotionally aware you are, it is still possible to find yourself controlled in the way Betty controlled me.

Betty over-salted and poured vinegar into my food. My house was no longer my own; uncles, aunts, cousins showed up unexpectedly. I was the odd one out, the alien in the family; I just didn't fit in. I refused to join Betty's boys and their father in their competitions to see who could make the most noise breaking wind. I did myself no favours by withdrawing more and more as time went on.

Fern loved TV wrestling; she would whoop and cheer along with Betty as a pair of muscle-bound morons cavorted in a badly choreographed 'fight'. Determined to keep Mahtob from these outlandish goings on I took her into the garden. Betty flew into a rage. "What's the goddamn matter? Let her watch, it's normal!"

Despite everything I loved Betty and could not imagine life without her – besides, I would never leave Mahtob, no matter what. But then a sudden, tragic death changed everything.

Chapter Sixteen
THE LAST OUTING

What on earth did this mean? Why had Betty seen someone from the Swiss Embassy? Betty had made a few female American friends and some of them had husbands who worked at the embassy. They visited each other's homes and went on trips together. But this sounded like something official. Whatever the reason, I'd had enough. I decided we would have to return to America and if Betty continued to ruin my relationship with Mahtob I would sue for divorce. With Betty's history of violent psychosis I thought I had a shot at winning a custody battle.

I still wasn't sure, however. Despite everything I still loved Betty and I hated the thought of what Mahtob would have to go through.

"What's the matter?" Betty asked me. "What's happened that makes you suddenly wanna go back?" I told her about my conversation with Miss Shaheem. "Aw her, she's just up tight. Shamsi visited me at school and Miss Shaheem freaked out." Again she begged me to stay in Iran, urging me to be patient. "I truly swear I will never fight with you again"

We had befriended Shamsi, an Iranian woman who lived part of the year in the USA. She confirmed Betty's story about the school. I reconsidered. Apart from our relationship, things were going pretty well. Work at the hospital was never-ending, full of drama, excitement and heartbreak as I rushed to treat severely wounded soldiers; sometimes it was like being in an episode of MASH, although unlike Hawkeye and the rest of his team, I felt as if I were really making a difference in difficult circumstances.

Mahtob loved her school and was top of her class. When Mahtob's teachers told us that she was their star pupil, Betty remarked - without irony - that "She got her brains from her American side," I found myself biting down hard on my tongue.

We employed a housekeeper and our social lives improved; Betty became close friends with Alice, an American woman married to an Iranian university professor. We had even started planning a family trip to the US to see Betty's family. Yet again, I decided to give both Betty and Iran one more shot.

As Christmas approached, I tried to find a tree (Christmas wasn't celebrated in Iran but of course I wanted it for Mahtob). I had became quite pally with our garbage collector and asked him if he could help. He somehow found a beautiful pine tree and we invited all our American friends for a New Year's Eve party. It was a great occasion, Betty's friends, including Ellen, Shamsi and Zari, all came and Mahtob was so happy and excited. Even Betty seemed happy, full of nervous excitement and I hoped that the New Year would bring happiness to us all.

We'd been planning a family trip back to the US that summer but this visit took on a new urgency when Carolyn, Betty's sister phoned on 24 January. Harold was very sick with cancer and she wanted my advice. I called Carson City Hospital and spoke to my old colleagues doctors only to be told that Harold was dying, that he had about five months at best.

When I broke the news to Betty; she seemed strangely reluctant to go and see Harold. "It's not as if he's dying this week," she said. This comment, although it sounded strange to me, was true enough but I said there was no reason why she couldn't leave now. We agreed it was important that Mahtob finish the school term - which was nearly over - and that I would follow with Mahtob. It was only right that Harold and Mahtob should be with one another one last time and although we'd not always been on the best of terms, I felt I owed Harold my last respects.

I called the travel agent and asked them to find some flights to Lancing, Michigan via Corpus Christi for Betty (we needed to check on the state of our house, which we'd rented out) and told her to choose among them herself. I signed the necessary permissions for my family to travel and made sure the travel agent knew we needed to book another twenty kilos in excess luggage for Betty's trip – we had collected a lot of gifts for the family since we'd been in Iran.

Shortly after this, Mahtob told me that her teacher had asked them to buy some school things for the kids from poor neighbourhoods. Together, we braved the snowy streets and bought coloured pencils and sharpeners, and an eraser shaped like a little doll. It was a rare moment of togetherness, a simple experience, nothing spectacular but joyful nonetheless.

It was the last outing I would ever have with my little girl.

CHAPTER SEVENTEEN

A FATAL ERROR

I sprinted through the corridors, skidding round corners; a child had been over-anaesthetised. As I ran my pager continued to scream its emergency call, but by the time I arrived, it was too late.

The dose, given by a member of my nursing team, was too massive for any human, let alone a child. She was on my staff - I was the consultant on call and it was my responsibility - so I had to resign and the hospital agreed, telling me they would have fired me if I hadn't gone voluntarily.

Betty found a local lawyer who advised me to sue the hospital; I wasn't sure, but they both convinced me there was nothing I could have done differently and the hospital shouldn't have accepted my resignation. To my amazement, Betty and the lawyer filed a lawsuit for $15 million.

Just days before the trial, the lawyer called me to say the hospital would settle for $100,000 and I agreed - anything to get the sorry business over with. The whole experience left a bad taste in my mouth. We didn't really need the money and I wasn't altogether surprised to learn that much of this extraordinary sum was taken up by the lawyer's fee.

The lawsuit made it difficult for me to find work locally. I was seen as trouble and once people knew I was Iranian my application would somehow find its way down to the bottom of the pile.

I eventually found work as a general practitioner in Detroit. It was a three-and-a-half-hour drive, too far to commute every day so I rented a tiny apartment, returning home at weekends. I tried to persuade Betty to move but she preferred to stay near her family and it was only natural that she didn't want to leave our idyllic home. While I was away her family stepped up its anti-Moody campaign. I'd return home to a bad-tempered Betty who tried to keep Mahtob away from me.

If she found me cuddling her or reading a story, she would drag Mahtob to her room, arguing that she was tired and needed to sleep. I'd done nothing wrong but it felt like we were divorced and I was the absent father.

It carried on like this for about a year. One week, I took an extra day off work and arrived home earlier than expected. As I walked in the door, Betty screamed - a man wearing a dark suit was walking up the drive towards the house behind me.

"What is it?" I asked, worried.

"Lock the doors and windows!" Betty yelled. "That man, he's been hanging around he house, I'm sure he's a burglar!"

"What? That's ridiculous."

Betty started to shake. I was exhausted from the long drive and couldn't bear the thought of her having a manic episode, so I played along, hoping it would wear off. We crouched behind the door as he buzzed, knocked, then left.

It was around this time that one of my many nephews, Mohammed Ali, came to stay with us. He had come to the USA to study for a Masters degree. He lasted just three days before Betty drove him away.

Life was bleak and confusing. Whilst everyone else in our house – Betty, her parents, her children and relatives had rights, I had none. I didn't think about separation or divorce. I wanted Mahtob to grow up in a family with both of her parents, enjoying the sort of childhood that I had never had. At the same time I just didn't know how much longer I would be able to cope. Suddenly, events in Iran suggested a possible solution.

I called my family in Iran regularly from my small apartment in Detroit. Now with Betty's family on the attack, ostracising me in my own home, I needed my own family even more, especially my beloved sister Ameh. It was wonderful to talk to Ameh who begged me again and again to come and see her - it had been ten years since I had last been in Iran for a brief visit, and I had been in no hurry to return – but now my sister's pleas moved me.

The war put a stop to many Iranians' growing unease with the revolution. There had been so many executions of former Shah supporters as well as 'counter-revolutionaries.' All their trials were held in secret but were all openly announced in newspapers, sometimes there were grim, grainy photographs of the hanged, silhouetted against a bright sky. Repression and censorship was a new fact of everyday life. Evin prison awaited newspaper editors foolish enough to print critical stories.

But thanks to the conflict with Iraq, Iranians couldn't afford to rail against the revolution. The war had united Iran where the revolution had so far failed. It was during these times that one had to support one's government, at least until the war had been won. Better the current government than Saddam Hussein.

Ayatollah Khomeini turned the defense of Iran in to a holy battle for our freedom. It was a hard concept to resist. We were outgunned by Iraq, our invader, who was able to call on its Western allies to give them missiles and cash, cash that Saddam Hussein spent on chemical weapons bought from European companies.

So, we put our worries about the revolution on the backburner and focused on the main problem at hand – which was once again the struggle for our *haq*, our right to a free and peaceful life.

This holy battle idea quickly migrated to the battlefield as military operations were given religious names and bases were named after Iran's holiest sites, including Karbala and Qods.

The problem for Iranians – particularly young, able-bodied male Iranians was that our only advantage over our better-armed opponent was sheer body of numbers. I remember weeping at the TV pictures on the news that showed teenagers marching bravely to the front to die a hideous death on a scale not seen since the First World War.

As a result, martyrdom became a fact of Iranian daily life. Television and radio became totally dominated by tales of the glorious dead, while the newspapers were full of columns of mourning; grief permeated the air like a heavy, invisible smog and the nation could do nothing but breathe it in.

I felt it just as keenly in America, thousands of miles away. Iraq was my homeland and I felt appalled for my countrymen as any expat would. Nothing hurt me more however, than when I learned the heartbreaking news that Khorramshahr, that paradise of my childhood, had fallen to Iraq on October 26 1980 - just three months after the war had started.

The glittering city of Khorramshahr had once been a bustling port with a population of 150,000. After several weeks of fierce house-to-house fighting, it had been gutted and turned into a ghost town of rubble fallen trees, telegraph poles, blackened vehicles and an enormous port that had all but been obliterated during the initial Iraqi bombardment. Broken dockside cranes tilted into the water, charred loading containers sat useless and empty, their contents treated as booty by Iraqi soldiers.

Even the railway station had failed to escape destruction. Oh, how well I had known and loved that railway station! Now the only people that stood on the platform were clusters of tired Iraqi soldiers who awaited not trains but news of plans of the next attack on the larger city of Abadan, just seven miles away.

Our poorly equipped soldiers had fought to the end; even after their guns failed and the ammunition ran dry they fought to the death with knives and clubs from one building to the next. Once they'd been pushed across the Karun River by the Iraqi onslaught, some Revolutionary Guards tried to sneak back under cover of darkness to set up sniper posts. Their simple plan was to slay as many Iraqi soldiers as they could before they were taken out. They didn't last for long.

Khorramshahr became our equivalent of the Russian city of Stalingrad, the last great city to fall to the Nazis in WWII. Although this is a massive simplification, the Russians had to make a stand and retake Stalingrad otherwise the Nazis would march straight into Moscow. It took two million lives but the Russians were victorious and the Nazis all-but perished in the Russian winter.

The Imam rallied the nation to retake Khorramshahr from the invader. This was the make or break moment for Iran. Lose and the country would fall. Win and we would send the Iraqi soldiers fleeing back across the Shatt al-Arab, ending the war.

The Iraqis meanwhile, were planning to move on to the larger city of Abadan. The city was all but surrounded; Iraqi troops were barely two kilometres from the centre of town. The city would be starved before the assaults would begin. Further into Iran the invader threatened to come.

These were desperate times and the Pasdaran answered the call. Before dawn in 24 April 1982 the cry "Ya Mohammad ibn Abdullah! Ya Mohammad ibn Abdullah!" signalled the start of the most ambitious operation of the war: the retaking of Khorramshahr, officially known as Operation Beit ol-Moqaddas.

Some 70,000 Pasdaran launched one of the bloodiest and most ambitious counterattacks the world has ever seen. It went better than anyone dared hope; in a few hours, two Iraqi divisions and two border guard brigades had been surrounded and taken prisoner while the rest of the Iraqi force of about 12,000 men was in full flight. Some were so desperate to escape that they jumped straight into the Shatt al-Arab and struck out for the Iraqi shore.

By this time the war had already cost Iran and Iraq an estimated 100,000 lives and $150 billion. So many men had been killed that the Ayatollah dubbed the city 'Khooninshahr' - 'City of Blood'.

I had been following these events breathlessly, and rejoiced. My city, my home town had been liberated! In Tehran, thousands took to the streets chanting "Allahu akbar" (God is great). Drivers honked their horns even more frequently than normal, and mosques filled with joyful citizens who wanted to offer thanks to God.

My rejoicing was short lived, however. I wept again when I saw images of the now ruined city and the many that had fallen. Because we won the battle, May 24 (the official date when it was certain Iran had total control of the city) is celebrated as the Liberation of Khorramshahr in Iran, while the Iraqi's celebrate Martyr's day. Every year, I mourn rather than celebrate the miserable foolishness of a war forced upon us by our leaders.

At the time we thought that now the war could at last end. The nation had been in agreement with the war until we had retaken Khorramshahr. Now we had won – at great human cost - a political and military victory. Saddam's army – which had better weapons and better-trained soldiers now realized they were never going to defeat a neverending army of millions of soldiers who would march over minefields to defeat the invaders.

Saddam Hussein had started the war with the specific aim of seizing part of our oil-producing Khuzistan province. He had hoped to become the region's strongman, but after Khorramshahr Iran regained nearly all of Khuzistan, and Iranian guns along the Shatt al Arab were now shelling Iraq. Saddam, who had wanted to weaken Khomeini's Islamic regime, was now in serious danger himself. Indeed, the month after Khorramshahr had been retaken, Saddam offered a truce.

But any hopes we had of peace were quickly dashed. Parliamentary Speaker Ali Akbar Hashemi Rafsanjani, who went on to become the fourth President of Iran, made it painfully clear with an expression of *haq*: "We shall stop at nothing in order to gain our legitimate rights, and the fall of Saddam Hussein is our greatest right."

The more radical advisors of the Imam urged him to seize the opportunity as they saw it, to push Iran into Iraq to unseat Saddam and claim tremendous power in the Middle East as a result. It was decided that this lunatic policy was the best way forward and soon, Iranian soldiers were pushing over the border.

My heart sank. It quickly became clear to me that Iran was desperate for doctors. The Iran-Iraq War was fought in the desert from trenches; young men, teenagers were being brought home from the front line in their hundreds every week, the victims of mustard gas, mines, snipers and heavy artillery – 400,000 men were in the battle zone (the war lasted eight years, leaving 500,000 Iranian soldiers dead or seriously wounded – it was about the same again for Iraq). As the weeks became months and then the months became a year, I read time and again about their suffering in the news and heard more about the horrors of war from my family.

I felt ashamed; tens of thousands of brave young men were making terrible sacrifices while I was enjoying a life of ease in the USA. I had become a doctor to follow in my parent's footsteps. They had given their lives treating British and American soldiers and here I was, living a life of comparative ease, growing rich and fat putting people to sleep. While many Iranians in the US seemed glad to be out of Iran, I was suddenly overcome with desire to go back. Imagine if this was happening to your country; could you sit by idly, watching and doing nothing? I desperately wanted to honour my parents and my countrymen.

I wondered…Betty had once said she would live anywhere in the world with me and so I decided I had nothing to lose. I would ask her to come to Iran for a year. Besides, who were we to deprive Mahtob from knowing her Iranian family? I also hoped that a new start away from the influence of the Love family would go some way towards healing our relationship.

It came as no surprise to me when Betty didn't take to the idea. "Iran!" she exclaimed, "What you goddamn thinking of, Moody? Think I want to go to a country where they kill Americans? Forget it."

Although I should have suspected it, I returned to Detroit a broken man. Iran had been a tiny light at the end of a very long, dark tunnel and now it was gone.

I was therefore astounded and delighted when, the following weekend, Betty brought up the subject of visiting Iran.

"If we come and live with you in Detroit," she said quietly with a soft smile, "we could plan a trip to Iran."

"Really?" I asked, utterly incredulous. "Why, what made you change your mind?"

"Well, you must miss your family. And after all we'll be comfortable won't we?"

"Of course! They're very wealthy and Iranian hospitality is the best in the world."

I didn't dare question Betty any further as to why she had changed her mind; I was terrified she would change it back again so I planned our visit as fast as I could.

Betty suggested that we rent out our home while we were in Iran. I readily agreed. We had over $1million in assets and savings, and we left all of it in America, earning interest, ready for our return. All we had were a few possessions packed into our cases and $10,000 in cash, which I knew would be worth many times more on the Iranian black market.

On August 3, 1984 we landed at Mehrabad Airport, Tehran to be greeted by a sign that read: "You will never win, America!"

Chapter Eighteen
SEARCHING FOR MOONLIGHT

Early in February 1986, Mahtob called to me from her bedroom. She spoke in Persian, telling me she'd had a nightmare. I told her to not be frightened, that I would stay with her and keep her safe. Eventually, she dropped into a deep sleep. I kissed her on the forehead and left.

The following day, as Mahtob and I put the finishing touches to our snowman, an hour or so before we were due to go to our neighbours' for dinner, an ambulance screamed down our street. I was needed at the hospital. A chemical weapons attack had left many injured and one man was critical. Waving goodbye to Mahtob and Betty I ran to the vehicle and off we went.

An hour later, Betty called me at the hospital; she was wondering whether we'd still make dinner with the neighbours. The critical patient had been stabilised, intubated and was on a ventilator. "I'll be there in an hour," I said, checking the watch Mahtob had chosen for my birthday three years before.

When I got home, the house was empty. On the hall table was a hastily scribbled note from Betty. 'I've gone to some friends. I'll call later.' Odd, I thought. I checked with the neighbours and they hadn't seen any sign of Betty. Then the phone rang.

"You've forced us to remain in Iran," Betty spat at me angrily, "for all this time you've tormented us. Now, finally it's over!"

"Are you delirious?" I asked, "Where's Mahtob?"

"She's with me. Don't try to find us."

"Can I speak with her?"

"We're somewhere safe, but it's too late for talking. And don't try to contact the police. You wait 'til we contact you." The line went dead.

I searched the house. Betty's jewellery box was empty. Then I opened our cash box where we kept most of our Iranian money. It was empty. Tears streamed down my face. Why had I listened? How could I have been so stupid? Would I ever see Mahtob again? Who would harbour Betty?

For a moment I thought there was a chance they had been kidnapped; it was not unheard of. I had to tell the police. I rushed into town and filed a missing persons report. I returned home and searched the house again – this time I discovered that all our photo albums were gone, the negatives too. Despair washed over me; life without Mahtob was just too hard to imagine and I broke down.

I was brought to my senses by my two nephews, Majid and Mohammed Ali, who came to help me look. As we left, we bumped into the garbage collector. Spotting my tears, he asked, "What's wrong, is there anything I can do to help?"

"My wife and daughter are missing, nobody knows where they are"

"What?" he said in surprise, "But I've just seen them; they're at Shamsi's house! I saw them when I was collecting their garbage."

Shamsi had been acting strangely. Just a couple of days ago she'd been over for dinner and cornered me in the kitchen. "Why are you forcing Betty to leave the country?" she'd asked. "I'm not," I replied, puzzled at her odd question, "She's planning to see her dying father. If you're worried, why don't you ask Betty?"

I rushed back inside our house and dialled her number. Shamsi answered. "The garbage man's told me Betty and Mahtob are with you!" I blurted. "Is it true?"

For a second Shamsi was lost for words. "I'm sorry, you've just woken me," she said, "I haven't seen them. The garbage man is mistaken."

I raced to Shamsi's house but there was no sign of Betty or Mahtob. Then I remembered - Betty's school visitor. If Shamsi was lying to me now then maybe... I drove to the US Interests Section of the Swiss Embassy. They turned me away claiming to know nothing about Betty. I went home and waited by the phone while my nephews combed the city.

I jumped up in hope when Mohammed Ali returned but he'd had no luck. He placed his hand on my shoulder and sat me down. "Look, I want you to think about something. Betty thinks only of herself."

"What do you mean?" I asked. Mohammed Ali glanced down at the floor, embarrassed.

"She may have run off with another man," he said.

I was dumbfounded; the idea had never even occurred to me and I told him to stop talking nonsense. Mohammed Ali looked at me for moment before staring down at his feet, his lips pressed tightly together as if he were biting his tongue.

The following morning, the new white car I had ordered was finally delivered. I imagined the happy scene this should have caused, Mahtob laughing, me driving, Betty by my side. My heart ached.

With still no word from the authorities, I tried calling Betty's family again. If Betty was planning to run away, surely they would know something. I rang and rang and rang until finally, Betty's sister, Carolyn, answered: "They've left Iran and I guess they ain't comin' back." All she would tell me was that Betty and Mahtob had left Iran but weren't in America, so there was no point me looking for them. But where else would they go? They must be in America. That was it. I had to return to the US. I searched for my passport but I couldn't find it anywhere – I ransacked the whole house but all I could find was my green card. As I stared at it, I noticed something. I picked it up.

My green card had expired – the day before.

CHAPTER NINETEEN
LOST WITHOUT MY DAUGHTER

"Permission can only be granted if your wife comes with you and signs the documentation, Dr Mahmoody," the official said dryly, "otherwise you will not receive a visa.

"But my wife's in America!" I yelled.

"There's no need to shout. She'll have to come here for you to go there."

"This is ridiculous! My wife has kidnapped our daughter!" Trying to put it in language they would understand, I said in desperation: "An Iranian child has been abducted by an American!"

It was no use. All was lost. Applying for a duplicate passport in Iran is still a lot harder than in any Western country. The government has always been extremely cautious when it comes to international travel and the authorities like to be totally satisfied that you really have lost your passport and didn't sell it.

At the passport office I found the most senior person I could and engaged them in what was the most frustrating tarof of my life.

'I am at your disposal should you need anything,' he told me.

He most certainly wasn't.

I asked about the progress of my passport application.

'It is going through the usual channels. Please do call in again if you need anything else.'

Of course this really meant 'Please don't bother us again but if you do then I will repeat exactly what I've said here, wasting both my time and yours.'

In reply, I said: 'I appreciate the fact that you have given up so much of your valuable time to see me.'

He beamed back at me benignly. His desk was clear, the office was quiet. No one had interrupted our short meeting.

'You've been very helpful,' I added, hoping to at least get a glimmer, a clue of some indication as to whether he understood the urgency of my application.

He wished me a safe journey home.

This kind of tarof is one of the main reasons why it is nigh impossible to penetrate Iran's bureaucracy; it makes it very easy for the bureaucrats to avoid doing anything they don't want to. Shouting and screaming didn't do me any good either.

My family had contacts within the bureaucratic walls of the foreign ministry and delicate enquiries there revealed that I would have to prepare myself for a good six months of filling out forms and attending interviews.

As my application for a new passport crawled its way through the bureaucratic nightmare, it was soon made clear to me that my application for a visa for the US was a hopeless case – especially when I learned that I needed a 'letter of support' from Betty. They also told me they would need to speak to us both. Without my wife, I had no good reason to travel to the USA – I wasn't a student any more and the restrictions for Iranians wishing to travel and stay for any length of time in the West had multiplied in the years since the Shah had been deposed and since I'd been back in Iran.

The US didn't have an embassy in Iran (it still doesn't at the time of writing) and it was left to the US Interests Section of the Embassy of Switzerland to act as the US protecting power. I wasn't a US citizen. Neither US passports nor visas to the United States were issued in Tehran. Without my wife's help, getting a US passport was going to be impossible.

I kicked myself for not applying for US citizenship while I was in the USA but I'd simply never gotten round to it. I didn't feel like I needed to. I *felt* American – I had married an American and I had my green card, a thriving business and did my part for the country by paying plenty of tax.

I was totally stuck.

I went to see my nephew Majid to talk it over. Perhaps he could go to America for me, I wondered.

Majid shook his head sadly at the suggestion. "It will do no good. It's all part of her plan, uncle."

"What do you mean Majid?"

"Can't you see? I'm sorry Uncle but you've blinded yourself to everything that's going on around you. Maybe I will understand one day what it's like when I fall in love, but for now you need my eyes to tell you what's really going on around you. I've been biting my tongue but now I have to tell you this for your own good."

I sat disconsolately as Majid told me what I already suspected in my heart to be true.

Betty had been planning her exit for some time and had made sure there would be no way I'd be able to chase after her. She had run away from twice before when we were in America and on those occasions I'd been able to bring her home - this time I had no chance.

"What can I do?" I asked Majid plaintively. "What do I do next?"

To that, Majid had no answer, although I expect the words he was on the verge of saying but didn't to spare my feelings, would have gone something like: "Nothing Uncle. You stay in Tehran and get on with your life."

Of course, it was never going to be that simple.

CHAPTER TWENTY
THE SCUD STRIKE

The days became weeks and still not a word from anyone. A cold depression gripped me and I stopped work. I was no good to anyone; a pathetic man full of self-pity, nothing anyone said or did could rouse me.

Meanwhile, the war with Iraq raged on; the skies of Tehran came to be menaced more and more by unpredictable missiles. The land-war had reached stalemate and to try and tip the balance, the Iraqis had invested in hundreds of Scud missiles.

The roar of Iraqi fighter planes and the explosions of Scuds became the soundtrack of our lives. It got so bad that some days as many as twenty rockets would hit the city and I was glad that Mahtob was safe in America. I would most definitely have left with Mahtob and Betty at this point if they were still here. Although the odds of being hit in a city of ten million were still very small, it was nonetheless a very real and frightening risk.

The Iraqi military announced that while they did not want to kill civilians, they would continue to bomb our cities in an effort to persuade our leaders to accept a ceasefire. To try and minimize deaths, they said, they would warn us in advance which areas the rockets were likely to fall and it would be up to us to get out of their way. So we awoke to check the warnings broadcast on the news as to which districts would be bombed that night; it felt like a truly perverse lottery. Some people fled but many stubbornly ignored the warnings, which as it turned out, were shockingly inaccurate. It became a macabre national joke that Iraqis couldn't read maps.

Driving through Tehran each morning, I occasionally saw a new small area of destruction, another building gone in the missile lottery. Despite our attempts at humour, the city was full of tension at this time.

A few weeks after the Iraqi army's announcement, I was at home, looking out of the window and wallowing in my misery, when the air-raid sirens alerting the city to approaching missiles started to wail.

I looked up and prayed for a Scud to hit me.

There was a blinding flash; a moment of silence as everything seemed to suck inwards, as if taking a breath - and then the world exploded. Doors and windows blew open; I was knocked to the ground as dust, dirt and plaster rained down on me.

Eventually, everything was still again, except for the swirling dust. I shook my head; everything sounded like it was underwater – dull, distorted, compressed. I tried to stand and to my relief I found that – apart from a few cuts – I was uninjured. I coughed handfuls of dust out of my lungs.

As I did so, my hearing started to return and I heard a high-pitched sound -children screaming. I staggered to the window. The Scud had landed close to a children's birthday party. I stood frozen in shock for a few moments, listening to the uncontrolled wails, staring at the devastated buildings in the street outside before I ran from my apartment.

I tried to jump down the stairs but as they were covered in rubble I was forced to clamber awkwardly before falling through the building's smashed doors and into the street. I crossed the road, putting on my doctor's professional head, readying myself for the worst, bracing myself for the horrors by turning them into medical cases that needed to be fixed.

I ignored the children that were awake and crying, rushing first to check the still, silent bodies who might need even more urgent attention. My guess was that they were all around the same age as Mahtob. I slammed the thought to one side.

'Focus!' I told myself. 'No time for your misery now, idiot!'

The first child's arm was twisted at a hideous angle, a massive fracture. She was lying on her back, her eyes closed. As I lifted the back of the head I felt the bone of her skull move and my hand came away wet. There was no pulse. I moved to the next motionless child. He was lying on his front, his back was ripped open; I could see the shock of white shoulder bone amongst the bright red. No pulse. There was nothing to be done.

I looked across what had once been the interior of a house, which now resembled a courtyard, roofless and open to the sky.

There were fifteen more tiny bodies lying still.

I cursed this stupid, stupid war for the ten thousandth time.

I ran from one child to the next, not even pausing to close the eyelids of those beyond help. Some I didn't have to go near to know that God had claimed them. I saw a pair of adult legs sticking out from a pile of rubble; if they were alive then they would have to hold on somehow until help arrived. If I spend any time digging them out, I thought, then I might miss the chance to save a child's life.

I found five children that I thought could be saved. They were all in the same area and it seemed as though their location, in a hallway between two thick stone walls, had saved them from the worst of the blast.

A girl in a dark green dress was out cold and had two bad fractures to her legs. The rest were all boys, one was unconscious and had stopped breathing but he came to back with a little gentle mouth-to-mouth resuscitation. He woke and the first thing he did was smile at me – a moment I still see with razor sharp clarity.

'Hi,' I said, 'There's been an accident. You need to lie still. Okay?' The boy, still smiling, nodded. I could see no obvious injuries and so moved on.

I cleared airways, staunched blood, and bound wounds with torn strips of cloth. All of them were burned to varying degrees. They would need skin grafts.

Now came the screams from adults. Parents, some of whom I knew by sight - I had watched them playing with their children in the parks. Now those happy days were gone forever. They came, running to that unlucky house from all over the neighbourhood to begin the dreadful search. When they found their child –the grief came out unadulterated, the low hollow moans, the shocked shrieks and wracking sobs.

"I'm sorry, I'm sorry," I found myself saying, as if it was my fault, as if I should have been able to save them.

I tried not to look as men and women tore at their hair and beat their chests. I tried not to hear the howls.

The familiar sound of sirens brought me round. As usual, the paramedics had fought their way through Tehran's congested, narrow and labyrinthine streets to reach the injured in record time.

I went back to check the little boy that I'd brought round and saw with rising dread that he was out cold again. I listened to his chest - no movement. I tapped it. It felt solid, heavy. Lifting his shirt I saw small cuts between his ribs. Blood and viscous liquid seeped through. Shrapnel.

His lungs were filling with fluid and were on the verge of collapsing. He needed a chest tube. I could hear the sirens drawing closer. Mouth to mouth had saved him last time, before his lungs had filled with fluid. Now it seemed as though the air had entered the lungs and not left, thanks to the fluid.

I'd heard of war surgeons doing chest tubes in the field using a knife and bits of pipe or rubber tubing washed in alcohol but I couldn't risk doing this myself here and now. I didn't even have a knife. But then even paramedics didn't put in chest tubes – that's a job for a doctor.

Tapping the chest I judged where the fluid was. At least I'd be ready.

When the first ambulance finally arrived and the paramedic climbed out I yelled for a thoracentesis needle. He pulled it out of his bag and ran towards me and I lifted the child and the needle went in the back and – air hissed.

The paramedic bent over his mouth. 'I think it worked,' he said.

I rode with them to hospital in a frantic, gut wrenching journey that was like being on the back of a boat in a raging storm as the driver hawed the weighty vehicle through Tehran's streets.

All of those five somehow pulled through. I was sick and shaking from the horror but felt alive again.

The paramedic bumped into me afterwards. Baggy-eyed we exchanged tired hellos and I updated him.

'Can I give you a lift home?' he asked.

'No thanks,' I said. 'I'm going to walk.'

The morning air was cooler than it had been in recent days but I could feel the sky already starting to boil under the rising sun. My mind was in turmoil.

How could I have stopped working? 'Yes, my heart may be broken,' I thought, 'but last night it soared with purpose. My head may be full of miserable thoughts but my knowledge is intact.'

I had a use; I was selfish not to apply it. I decided then that medicine would be my life's purpose. I would carry on with life and I would allow myself to hope that one day I would see Mahtob again.

CHAPTER TWENTY ONE
ARMISTICE

I threw myself back into my work, and treated the victims of war without rest, spending as little time as possible at home. The attacks escalated; Iraq launched 226 sorties over 42 days, bombing civilian neighbourhoods, once hitting a primary school and killing 65 children in one terrible, terrible day.

I bent over the suffering children than poured through the doors and into the operating room and put them to painless sleep. I said a prayer each time, asking that the surgery would save them and that I would see them afterwards, to help make their recovery as pain-free as possible.

After that was over, thirty-six hours since the first child burst through the hospital's doors, I stepped exhausted into the street, pulling on my coat.

'Dr Mahmoody.'

I turned to see the ambulance driver that had been first to arrive the night of the Scud strike.

'How about some tea before you go home?'

I hadn't wanted to share the company of another person since Mahtob left and usually I would have said no without a second's thought. This time I paused. We had been through something important together, something that had affected us both enormously and I decided that yes, some company would be most welcome.

'Why not?' I said. 'I'd be honoured.'

From that terrible tragedy our friendship was born. Amin was a good fifteen years younger than me. He'd lost many friends in this nonsensical war, a war in which he'd worked as a frontline medic before being sent home, his time served to continue as a city ambulanceman.

Amin was the first person outside of the family I talked about Betty and Mahtob as a friend. It helped. Opening up to Amin made me phrase my thoughts a certain way – in a way I hadn't before. He helped me see where I'd gone wrong in our relationship in the lead up to the disaster – my own family after all, couldn't help but be biased and blamed Betty simply to make me feel better. Although he pushed me hard enough to make me walk away on several occasions, Amin proved to be my first true friend.

Amin also opened up to me. He told me of his experiences as a medic in the war. Eventually, after having gone far beyond the time he was meant to serve, full of battle fatigue, he was sent back to Tehran where he returned to work as a paramedic and now, instead of gassed soldiers he collected the victims of missile attacks.

One day, he introduced me to his brother, Hussein, who had fought on the front lines in the latter part of the war. His experience was typical of hundreds of thousands of young Iranian men.

'Like you, I was also hit by a bomb,' Hussein told me as we drank tea in one of the many cafes near the hospital, 'more than once. When the call came, my brother and I packed out things and set out for the front – he as a medic, me as a soldier - our mother weeping after us, imploring us to stay or to run away.

'A few weeks later I was in uniform carrying my helmet, pack on our back containing chemical and biological bags, a water canteen and, of course, my gun at my side.

'My best friend in that war was a man called Hassan. He was an enormous man, fat but light on his feet; his patience and humour seemed to me to be endless and he was a much better soldier than I. Hassan was afraid but acted like a man without fear. Everybody else tried to back away from the front line but he always stood the ground he'd been ordered to defend or advance without question.

'My brave friend had a secret, and he only confided in me after I promised to never tell our comrades. "I never fire to kill," he said; "I would never shoot another human being. If they shoot me then it's God's will and I trust in God!"

'Many soldiers would have agreed with Hassan. But instead of standing their ground against the enemy, they preferred to desert – most took their chances in Iraq, and fled over the border in the hope that they would have a better chance as deserters and PoWs than staying in the slaughterhouse of war.

'Hassan never considered deserting as an option – even when our sergeant (who was honourable enough to tell us beforehand) disappeared into the desert and over the border one day.

'We lived in a mortar bunker, two rooms lined with sandbags and planks from ammunition crates in a hole in the ground with earth piled on top about a metre high. Our mortar shells came from North Korea and Israel but we'd recently been sent green and black missiles from our very own "Military Defence Industries".

'During one exchange of fire, a mortar shell passed over me and exploded in a depression behind the bunker. I dived inside as another one came down – it's deadly whistle stopped right above my head. I had a quarter of a second to say my final prayer before the shell exploded, levelling the trench, and burying me under a few feet of earth. I couldn't move for the weight of the soil and as I started to suffocate I felt hands clawing at my boots. Hassan drew me out choking in a fit of fear and panic.

'He dragged me to a shallow trench full of thorny bushes, so shallow it was more of a groove really, just a few metres south, the only place below the skyline. White-hot shrapnel whistled, zinged and hissed above our heads in between the ear-popping thuds of mortars as we lay there, waiting for the end; me hacking up my lungs, which were still full of dust, Hassan calmly lying on his back looking up at the sky. We survived, somehow, I don't know how, by the grace of God.

'I thought I was going to die so many times in that bloody, savage war. Thanks to the idiocy of our commanders, thirty of us ended up being pretty much surrounded in that stinking bunker, which we had to re-dig in another position in the desert's hard earth.

'Iraq had retaken a chunk of desert that we had taken from them three years before, and we had been sent to win it back in this never-ending push-me-pull-me war. According to the official radio reports broadcast in Tehran we'd already won the battle but in reality we'd fled the towns we'd held all-too briefly - thanks to the fog of poison gas that exploded from giant cans dropped onto no-man's land from the sky.

'Nothing puts wings on your feet faster than a cloud of approaching poison gas. A few of our men were sick after that attack but at least no one died. For some, that would come years later, first slowly sinking into blindness then having the breath sucked from their dying lungs – a slow, dark and suffocating end.

'Some suffered from the immediate effects, the massive blisters that popped before refilling with pus that ate away at the skin. At least they were sent home. Even our commanders weren't crazy enough to force those men back into a losing battle. Not good for morale for the rest of us to see them melting before our eyes.

'Just as bad as the threat of mustard gas was the presence of the National Liberation Army of Iran (NLA).'

The NLA were a fanatical and schizophrenic group of Iranians, also known as the Organization of the People's Holy Warriors of Iran, National Council of Resistance, The National Council of Resistance of Iran, the People's Mujahedin Organisation of Iran and the Muslim Iranian Students' Society.

Founded in 1965, the aim of this Islamic and Socialist group – apart from destroying capitalism and ending Western imperialism – was to violently overthrow the Shah of Iran. To this end they fought alongside supporters of Ayatollah Khomeini in the run up to and during the Iranian Revolution – often performing the less savoury tasks, such as rounding up prisoners and performing summary executions.

The NLA soon became infuriated with the new regime. For a start, the Imam's mullahs took the Shah's palaces after the overthrow, then cornered the black market and quickly on the road to becoming as rich as the Shah.

Receiving inadequate reward for doing the Imam's dirty work, the NLA wasted no time in switching targets and decided to overthrow Ayatollah Khomeini. They quickly started a program of assassinations and murdered a president, a prime minister and a chief justice before the conflict with Iraq became their Holy War.

They were fanatical ideologists and didn't seem to care much whether they lived or died – as long as they got to kill lots of Iranian soldiers first and so they joined forces with Iraq against their own country.

The NLA once took three thousand prisoners of war in just one battle near Mehran - including two colonels. They claimed tanks, armoured personnel carriers, American-made anti-armour missiles, cannons and mortars, hundreds of machine guns, and hundreds of light and heavy military vehicles.

'Stories of mass slaughter of thousands of prisoners travelled though the trenches faster than a desert rat,' Hussein continued, 'although there were some among us who sympathized with their aims and believed they would be merciful if we surrendered.

'The radio was always on. No one listened to the Iranian radio stations for news of the war, however. All they ever did – in-between broadcasts of monotonous patriotic songs – was tell epic tales of countless victories – so many false victories had been broadcast that it seemed impossible that we could not have won the war – or that a single Iraqi was left alive to fight it – rather than feeling like we were on the verge of total collapse. Listening to those broadcasts whilst watching your friends and comrades being wrapped in their funeral shrouds was enough to drive anyone insane.

'Our commanders forced us to listen to the "morale-boosting" (as they saw it) radio by placing speakers all about our bases and camps. Problem was they were so loud that the Iraqi artillery could hear them from their positions and they simply directed their rockets at the noise.

'I was standing right by a speaker, 'talking' to my friend Hassan, the man who saved my life (we had to yell to be heard). I jokingly told Hassan that his girth was drawing enemy fire. He laughed. "It's not my fault; God has made me this size," he said with a board smile. Just then a shell exploded right by us.

'When I came to, I saw Hassan's mighty feet, one boot on and one boot off sticking out of the back of an ambulance as it roared away to the med bay. He died later that night.

'It's hard to explain just how hellish it was. The heat. The sun even burned the orange and blue lizards that skitted across the desert floor. Our sweat turned our uniforms white with with crusty salt. There was no hope of a wash and we were miles from a well.

'It was on one such scorching day that the sergeant approached us and said: "I've been told to turn our 120mm mortars on any deserters in case they give away our positions under torture."

"I won't do it," I said.

"Calm yourself," the sergeant replied, "I too have no intention of doing carrying out such an order. The Iraqis can tell our positions anytime they like with their drones. I want to desert anyway. Do you know anyone who could get me to Kurdistan?"

'I shook my head. Another man, a friend of mine, nodded. He was taking a risk but he trusted our sergeant.

"How much?" the sergeant asked.

"Depends."

"On what?"

"Are you political?"

"Of course I'm political. I'm in the army and disagree entirely with the conflict."

'That's not enough. I know a man who might take you but you will have to pay. Politicals don't pay usually – unless they're wealthy politicals of course."

'Any plans of desertion were quickly put on hold the following July morning when the Iraqis started to bomb our positions – mainly with smoke bombs. We fired mortars back at them but they stopped five minutes later.

'They wanted us to fire so they could mark our positions,' the sergeant said.

'About one hour later, a small Iraqi plane flew overhead; it was returning to base after dropping gas on our HQ, to the north. We fired our anti-aircraft gun but it was too high. It was soon followed by a drone that cruised above us in a wide circle.

"We're lost," the sergeant observed, "That's their reconnaissance done, they'll knock out the big guns before bringing in the NLA to slaughter us all tomorrow."

'He was right but they came sooner than we expected; first more planes which quickly took out our best anti-aircraft guns, leaving columns of black smoke rising into the blue sky. We were truly helpless.

'A few minutes later the guns stopped shooting and the platoon fell. From there, the invasion could either go straight to the headquarters of the battalion or it could be diverted toward us.

'But of course they never came.'

On July 3, 1988, at 10.54am, the lives of 290 innocent people came to an abrupt end when a SM2- Standard Missile fired from the USS Vincennes destroyed Iran Air Flight 655. The US said that the ship's $600m Aegis system - the most sophisticated battle-managing array of radars, sensors, computers and automatically guided weapons ever put together - had mistaken the airliner for an F14 jet fighter flying towards the ship in attack mode, adding that it had ignored repeated requests to indentify itself. It was left to journalists to point out that the F14 was barely one-third the size of the passenger jet and that the Vincennes had the most sophisticated radar system in the world at its disposal.

Needless to say, images of the dead bobbing in the Persian Gulf did nothing to improve US-Iran relations. The fact that the US could barely bring itself to apologise – blaming instead the 'fog of war' before adding that no one would be punished for the error – did not help.

But what this did do was to signify to Iran that perhaps America was on the verge of getting involved in our war and our leaders decided, after almost eight years and one million lives, to end the fighting and accept a United Nations Security Council ceasefire resolution.

Ayatollah Khomeini made an historic announcement. 'I pledged to fight to the last drop of my blood,' he said, 'and though this decision is akin to drinking poison chalice, I surrender myself to the will of God.'

No one could believe that the war that had been with us for so long, the only reality many of our children had ever known, had come to an end. Suddenly we could stop focusing on whether or not there would be a missile strike tomorrow and instead take stock of the cost of war. It had been massive.

Our farmland and industrial heart had all but been destroyed; the war had begun before we'd had a chance to adjust to the revolution and now we had to somehow find a way of adjusting to peace under the revolution.

But it wasn't quite over yet. Six days after the ceasefire, the NLA dispatched 7,000 fighters from a base in Iraq to attack the western Iranian province of Kermanshah. On the eve of the operation called 'Eternal Light', the terrorist leaders promised their troops that the Iranian masses would join their fight and help them to victory.

How wrong they were.

The last thing Iranians wanted at that moment was more violence. And they would never forgive the terrorists for joining Saddam and killing Iranians. The Revolutionary Guards joined forces with the army – including Hussein - and crushed the terrorist offensive, killing nearly 2,000 fighters and sending others fleeing back over the mountains to Iraq.

Hussein made it through, returned to Tehran, rejoined his brother and tried to get on with his life. But, the violence continued even at home. It seemed as though we would never be free of slaughter.

In July 1988, after the last great battle with the NLA, the Imam issued a fatwa decreeing that 'those who are in prisons throughout the country and remain steadfast in their support for the Monafeqin (Mojahedin) are waging war on God and are condemned to execution.'

There were over 40,000 such prisoners in our jails. 'Death committees' made up of an Islamic judge, a representative of the Ministry of Intelligence, and a state prosecutor were created to decide which prisoners would be executed.

They would line up prisoners in a fourteen-by-five-metre hall in the central office building and then ask one simple question, 'What is your political affiliation?' Those who replied "Mojahedin," were hanged.

A great many stayed true to the Mojahedin.

In Evin prison, every half an hour from 7.30am to 5pm, more than thirty people, including children who were as young as thirteen, were lifted on three forklift trucks to six cranes, each of which had five or six ropes. In just two weeks, 8,000 people were hanged in Tehran alone.

Despite everything, all the daily horrors that took place in Tehran, a day didn't pass that I didn't think of Mahtob. Talking about what had happened to me with Amin helped but it certainly wasn't a cure. On those rare occasions I found myself home alone with time on my hands I kept glancing at the door, hoping Betty and Mahtob would walk through it and back into my life.

Life passed this way for months until that most unexpected day when a friend called me to say Betty was on TV.

CHAPTER TWENTY TWO
LECTURE OF A LIFETIME

I looked at the Tehran university students as I began my lecture, speaking from memory.

"The Zagros Mountains, parallel ranges of folded mountains, almost impassable when travelling from east to west, run some 1,100 miles, beginning near the Turkish border, southeast along the western border of Iran, down to the Strait of Hormuz. They form a range as high as the Alps and as broad as Switzerland.

"Many of the ranges crest at 10,000 feet or above and the Zard Kuh, which is the highest peak in the Zagros, is almost 15,000 feet high. Snow is common throughout the ranges in winter and some higher peaks remain snow-covered throughout the year.

"Huge salt domes - up to 5,000 feet high - are found near the centre of the mountains. Oil and bitumen seeps straight of the earth and sometimes spontaneously ignites. Naphtha – coal tar – also forms pools from underground springs. Animals found in the mountains include wild sheep and goats that are preyed upon by wolves, bears, hyenas and leopards.

"Twice every year, 500,000 men, women and children — along with one million animals — struggle for eight gruelling weeks to scale the Zagros Mountains to reach their summer pastures. This is the miracle that is the Bakhtiari migration, one of the most hazardous tests of human endurance known to mankind.

"In 1976, a documentary film called *People of the Wind* that was made about their journey. "

Images from the movie, a spectacular sight of rugged, snow-covered land sweeping for as far as the eye could see, played behind me as I spoke.

'The men, women and children literally pushed a million cows, goats and horses up seemingly sheer cliffs thousands of feet above nothing, mountains that would defy all but the hardiest European mountaineers.

'These people have been doing this for hundreds of years, and every year many of them are lost. Graveyards pepper the route, stones marked by carvings of the animals that the dead had driven before them.

'Here we see tribal leader Jafar Qoli telling the filmmaker about a time they were caught in a terrible storm. He says he carried an exhausted young woman on his back all night. When he lifted her down in the morning, he found that she had died.

'Now, let me ask you. Is this a suitable environment for a six-year-old-girl?

'If Betty loved her daughter so much then why risk her life? In her book and in the film, when Betty visits Helen at the US interests section of the Swiss Embassy in Tehran, she receives a dire warning about trying this. In fact, this is a key passage, from where the book gets its name. I will read it to you:

'*Helen added a story. Only recently an Iranian woman had attempted this escape route with her daughter, paying smugglers to take them across the border. The smugglers took them close to Turkey and simply abandoned them in the mountains. The daughter died of the combined effects of starvation and exposure. The woman finally wandered into a village, disoriented and near death. All of her teeth were missing.*

"Of all the ways out," Helen said, "through Turkey is the most dangerous." She suggested, "You could get a divorce. I can take you to United Nations and get you a divorce and permission to leave on humanitarian grounds. Then you would be allowed to go back to America."

"Not without my daughter!" I said sharply.

"You are crazy," Helen said. In front of Mahtob she added, "Why don't you just go and leave her here? Get out of this country. Just forget about her."

I could not believe Helen could be so callous to say this in front of Mahtob. She apparently did not understand the depths of the mother-child bond.

'Surely going to Turkey over the mountains was the most dangerous option? An option that would mean there was a good chance of Betty returning to America *without* her daughter.

'Betty even admits as much:

"I would die in the mountains separating Iran and Pakistan, or I would get Mahtob safely back to America."

'But if Betty dies, then Mahtob dies too. And then again, Betty says:

"Mahtob slept with the innocence of childhood, but for me there would be no rest until I got my daughter to America-or died trying."

'If Betty died in the Zagros Mountains, then what chance would Mahtob have? I know Betty and I am sure she would never take that chance with Mahtob.

'Betty was tough and smart but she had no appetite for such hardship or any wish to put Mahtob in such extreme danger. If I were to suggest a more practical way to get home than over the mountains then it would be this.'

A picture of Tehran airport appeared behind me.

'Now, I know that for some people, Mehrabad airport might be fraught with danger, but, with the right papers, which Betty had, it's not terribly difficult to walk in with an American passport, buy a Swissair flight to the US via Paris and a few hours later, as Betty put it: 'board the plane to America and fly home in comfort.'

'Our laws said she needed permission from her husband but I had already given Betty permission to fly to see her sick father. I mean, why wouldn't I? I had no idea what she was planning. Things hadn't been great between us but as far as I was concerned they weren't terrible either; relations had even improved a bit since Christmas and I fully believed we had a future together. Mahtob was at school, already the top of her class. It was mid-term and neither of us wanted to upset her progress – but this was her grandfather we were talking about. For all Harold's faults, he loved Mahtob and Mahtob loved him. I, on the other hand, was hardly Harold's biggest fan and although I felt sorry for him I did not want to return to America just yet. I was swamped with work at the hospital; I could not bring myself to leave at that moment and Betty supported the decision for Mahtob and I to follow on at the end of that term.

'Besides, I was free to come and go from Iran as I pleased, thanks to my passport and green card. Her father was genuinely ill, there was no mistake about that. I spoke to Betty's family and the doctors myself.

'I think Betty wanted to hang on until my green card expired. Even if I got a new passport to replace the one she'd taken, then getting back to the USA really was going to be all but impossible without *her* permission.

'I'm going to play you a key scene from the film. It's when Betty first goes to the US interests section of the Swiss Embassy to ask for help. You'll notice that Helen, as she is called in the book, is called Nicole here for some unknown reason:

Nicole: Why did you come to Iran?

Betty: {miming shock and confusion} I don't know {long pause, holds head in hands}. I don't know {holds head again}. I was afraid to come. I wanted to trust him. I was frightened to come but I never thought this would happen {pause}. I thought of him as an American {pause}. He's changed. Oh god he's changed.

It was a truly dire performance. I paused the tape at a point where Sally field looked especially confused.

'She looks like she's struggling to remember her lines!' A young man exclaimed, causing others in the lecture hall to laugh.

'Yes, you might be interested to know that while *People of the Wind* won an Oscar, *Not Without My Daughter* did not. In fact, it was criticised heavily for its portrayal of Iran by American critics.

'I would say that this is the dominant expression of Betty made by Sally Field throughout the entire movie, one of confusion and disbelief – at how appalling the script is. She seems to be struggling to speak her lines.'

There was more laughing. Many would have seen the film already and knew how terrible it was.

'But now we move onto the very next scene which features me, played by Mr Alfred Molina.'

Once again, the events unfolded behind me. As Betty and Mahtob arrive home late, my sister drags Mahtob away and I march quickly up to Betty and punch her in the face before hissing:

'You try anything like this again then I'll kill you.'

And then I'm gone.

'A number of things to say here. Of course I deny I ever struck Betty in such a way. Anyone who knows me will tell you that I am most certainly not a violent person. I abhor any violence. I was against the war for this reason.

'I wasn't even capable physically. Alfred Molina is 6ft 2.5in and Sally Field, you will notice is 5ft 2.5in.

'Both Betty and I are about the same height and, putting it politely, she is a broader lady than Sally Field. Forgive me, but she weighed more than I did. I've never been in the best of health, my shoulders are narrow. Is anyone here my height? Would you mind?'

A young lady came up and stood in front of me, smiling politely and somewhat embarrassed.

'Now I think you could fight me off quite easily – but don't worry I'm not going to ask you to! Your shoulders are broader, your arms are longer. I think I would soon be in trouble if I tried to box you. I don't think I would even reach your head.

'Forgive my sometimes flippant tone but this is more a critique of the book and the film, and not of Betty – and most certainly not of my beloved innocent Mahtob, nor do I wish to belittle the subject of violence against women, which is something I vehemently oppose. Believe me when I say this hurts – and nothing more so than the next scene I'm going to show you at one hour, fifteen minutes and thirty-seven seconds into the film.

'Betty and Mahtob have just returned from seeing the mysterious man who is going to help them 'escape' and he generously says to pay him later.'

I played the film. Molina was beating Field wildly in what was supposed to be a deadly serious scene at Mahtob's school but with the flailing arms of the giant Molina and the same scream repeated again and again by Betty, the students started to laugh. I paused the scene with Molina's face twisted in poorly-acted rage.

'And now let me read the description of a violent scene from the book:

"My outburst was cut short by the strength of Moody's clenched fist, catching me full on the right side of my head. I staggered toward one side, too stunned to feel the pain for a moment. I was conscious of Mammal and Nasserine entering the room to investigate the commotion, and of Mahtob's terrified shrieks and Moody's angry curses. The hall reeled in front of my eyes...

Mahtob tried to wedge herself between the two of us, but Moody pushed her aside roughly. Her tiny body slammed against a wall and she cried out in pain. As I turned toward her, Moody slammed me down onto the bed...

Moody clutched my hair in his left hand. With his free fist he pounded me again and again on the side of my head.

Mahtob raced to help and again he pushed her aside.

I struggled against his hold, but he was too powerful for me. He slapped me across the cheek with his open palm. "I'm going to kill you" he raged.

I kicked at him, freed myself partially from his grip, and tried to scramble away, but he kicked me in the back so viciously that paralyzing pains shot up and down my spine.

With Mahtob sobbing in the corner and me at his mercy, he became more methodical, punching me in the arm, pulling at my hair, slapping me in the face, cursing all the time. Repeatedly, he screamed, "I'm going to kill you! I'm going to kill you!"

'And then, after this supposed beating is over, Betty writes-'

Mahtob ran to me and buried her head in my lap. We shared our pain, not merely the physical bruises, but the deeper ache that lurked inside. We cried and gasped for breath, but neither of us was able to speak for many minutes.

My body felt like one huge bruise. Moody's blows had raised two welts on my head so large that I worried about serious damage. My arms and back ached. One leg hurt so badly that I knew I would be limping for days. I wondered what my face looked like.

'Do you think I am capable of such a feat? And how about here?'

"Weeping and screaming, fearful for my life as well as her own, Mahtob did not want to leave me alone with the madman named Daddy. She attacked him from behind with her tiny fists, pounding at him in futility and frustration. Her arms tugged at his waist, trying to pull him off of me. Angrily he swatted at her, slapping her easily off to the side...

...Moody bit into my arm deeply, drawing blood. I screamed, wriggled free from his grasp, and managed to kick him in the side. But this produced anger more than pain. He grabbed me with his two mighty arms and threw me to the hard floor. I landed on my spine and felt pains shoot the entire length of my body.

Now I could barely move. For many minutes he stood over me, cursing violently, kicking at me, bending over to slap me. He yanked me across the floor by pulling at my hair. Tufts came loose in his hands."

'I am described like an animal here. I bite her arms like a beast and – she describes my arms as 'mighty'!' I lifted my arms, much like a muscleman would. 'Well? What do you think of these?'

They started laughing. It has been the same for every lecture since. Whenever I show students the scenes of Molina attacking Field and Field fleeing across the mountains, they burst out laughing, simply because they are so ridiculous.

'Yes it is funny because to us it is unbelievable. But - the fact that people across the world did believe this, accepted that this is the normal behaviour of Iranian men hurts me like I hope you will never feel.'

'But how can anyone believe this?' a young man asked.

'Because it feeds into a stereotype that those in power have tried to feed their subjects. They don't understand Iran so they're afraid of Iran – afraid of what we might do to upset the world's oil supply perhaps, how we might effect economies around the world – many Americans still remember the gasoline shortages in 1973-4, caused by the Organisation of Petroleum Producing Countries[6].'

Again and again, from 1973 to 1974, the cartel, led by Saudi Arabia and closely supported by Iran, raised the price of oil until it reached unprecedented heights, leading to the greatest and swiftest transfer of wealth in all history: the 13 OPEC countries earned $112 billion from the rest of the world in 1973. For a while, Iran got rich from American dollars, UK pounds, German Deutschmarks and so on.

'As the price of oil and oil-based products increased, people spent less money on other things, leading to a reduction in imports and a slow down in world trade – putting most of the Western world in danger of recession.

'Unfortunately, we helped reinforce these stereotypes; we projected images and fed the US speeches that were designed to keep them at arm's length, lest they try and interfere in our country's affairs yet again. Thanks to previous history, and I'm thinking in particular of the CIA-backed coup of 1953 - our leaders saw what the USA was capable of and felt threatened by them.

'Besides that, the hostage crisis didn't help and neither did the fact that we ended up in war - through no fault of our own - with a Western-backed Middle East power. For a decade before this film we were already portrayed as a nation of crazed, backward and uncivilized people. In the book, my character is often described as being like all Iranian men.

'As we know, uncivilized people make up small percentage of every nation – even in the USA, a country that today has very high recorded rates

---

6 OPEC was made up of Saudi Arabia, Iran, Venezuela, Nigeria, Libya, Kuwait, Iraq, United Arab Emirates, Algeria, Indonesia, Qatar, Ecuador and Gabon

of domestic abuse, a country that executes its criminals by electric chair, lethal injection and firing squad.

'For us, watching this film today, it is the equivalent of a modern-day American audience watching 1950s anti-communist propaganda films. They are comically funny and paranoid; cartoon like in the portrayal of the Russians and suspected American communists. But the American audiences that watched these films in the 50s when the threat of Russia felt very real, and very close, reacted very seriously indeed. The same applies here. America feels as though we are a threat and so the badness of the movie is ignored in favour of the "true story" it portrays of the Iranian savage.'

Having answered the young man's question, I turned back to the screen. I showed clips of Field fleeing Tehran late at night, through streets full of men and women in chadors standing round oil drums and burning wood for heat (something I don't think any Iranian has ever seen), streets full of police vehicles sirens blazing, 'Goodness knows where they're all rushing at that time of night,' I said, causing more laughter.

After a series of car journeys and an overnight stay Field is driven into Turkey where, to the sound of triumphant bells, the first thing she sees, lo and behold (at 1:51.25) is the American Flag outside the US embassy. Field ends the movie with 'We're home baby, we're home.'

'It's sheer propaganda,' a female voice said.

'Yes, exactly. Once again the reality is quite different from the imagery we're being shown. And you will remember that this lecture is not simply to try and show that significant elements of Betty's story are wrong, but to show how the West has used the story she told to help build a larger false picture of our culture.

It is to do with fear - because Iran is, to them, a strange land ruled by an all-powerful religious leader. They would much rather we ran things like they did -but not so well that we could ever cause them any trouble, of course. I am talking about the nation's leaders here, feeding lies to their people. That's what I meant when I said that I think things got a bit beyond Betty's control.

Take for example this passage from the book, when Betty waits at school for Mahtob and, to pass the time, wanders the hallways:

"Maag Barg Amerika!" came the chant from every classroom. "Maag Barg Amerika! Maag Barg Amerika!" There it was again, drilled into the malleable mind of every student, pounding into the ears of my innocent daughter, the official policy of the Islamic Republic of Iran, "Death to America!"

Some of the students gasped incredulously when I read this passage.

'Of course this never happened. But the book portrays Iranians as if hatred is drummed into us from birth. And you might be interested to hear the book's further thoughts on the Iranian education system:

"There was no leeway, no room for independent thought or questioning or even inflection of voice. This was the schooling that Moody had received as a child. Musing upon this, I reached a better understanding of why so many Iranians are meek followers of authority. They all seemed to have difficulty making a decision."

'Well, what do you think about that?'

'I don't think we would be here if that was true!' a man called from the back of the hall.

'Of course! At least the filmmakers behind 'Not Without My Daughter' had the 'excuse' that they were – as far as they understood it anyway – protected by the phrase 'Based on a true story'. So they have the usual get-out that this is a semi-fictional adaptation.

The book however, is different. It states it is the truth of what happened but plays on every unpleasant racial stereotype going. I am going to ask you to remain calm, to not get angry with Betty, because I think events spiralled out of her control.

Betty once admitted in an interview with a French journalist that her story was written with the help of the bestselling author William Hoffer to make it more 'realistic' and 'exciting'.

Hoffer was also the co-author of *Midnight Express* (1977), which British filmmaker David Putnam (who adapted the book for film) later reportedly branded as a "dishonest work" once Turkey complained about the book and film's racist portrayal of its people.

In the first thirty pages of *Not Without My Daughter*, there are several overblown racist and untrue comments directed at my family and our home. For example, Betty says all Iranians are unhygienic, smell and don't wash; that our damp homes are full of huge cockroaches (repeated several times); that Iranians eat like starved wild animals, spilling and spitting food, dribbling it from our mouths over our clothes and back into the serving bowls (a claim she also feels compelled to repeat); that a disproportionate amount of children had deformities that were the result of inbreeding; that women wiped their noses on the veils they wore."

'The co-author, William Hoffer hit gold with *Midnight Express* in the 70's, so he stuck to his formula: Write - what is in my opinion - a sensational, over-dramatic, and one-sided, book that libels an entire nation. I don't doubt that he didn't believe it was true but his American bias, which was only natural, came into play and he unintentionally painted a false picture of our nation.

Iranians are described as an "unwashed humanity"; their expressions are "dim and void" and the country is backward, "yet to learn the lessons of basic hygiene and social justice."

She describes how diaper-less babies are allowed to crawl among cock-roaches, and then how they urinate and defecate on the carpets.

'Has anyone here seen anything like this in an Iranian home? Even the filmmakers weren't prepared to stretch their viewers' imaginations that far and so didn't include the 'unclean' scenes.

'It was in the book time and time again: *"Together we spent hours meticulously cleaning the bugs out of the rice before we cooked it."*

According to Betty's book, Iranian women kept whole animals, feathers and innards, in the freezer and refroze and thawed the same meat over and over again. Bugs and worms infested the rice – which was never washed before it was cooked and of course, cockroaches were everywhere.

'It's a wonder any of us are still alive!' a student exclaimed, causing much laughter.

'The book also attacks Iranian mothers:

"You are crazy," Helen said kindly. "Go to the police. Get out of the country that way. Leave Mahtob here."

..To her {Helen} children did belong to the father. She simply could not identify with my maternal instinct."

'Whose mother here lacks maternal instinct?'

'This is an outrage!' a female student cried out, and a bit of a hubbub followed. I continued once they had calmed down.

'This book was the most powerful propaganda tool that America could have wished for. It sold twelve million copies worldwide. Twelve million!

Very few books in history have sold so many. So it was a 'great book' in one sense. It was a political masterpiece; it was even nominated for the Pulitzer Prize! Why? Because it perfectly captured the political feeling of the day.

'Of course, the language of *Not Without My Daughter* has not dated well; it is full of racist lies about myself, my family, Iran and Iranians and our culture, religion and politics. I'm the first to admit that life in Iran during the war was far from perfect; I too found it difficult to adjust, coming from America to my home that had drastically changed after the revolution. Having said that, we were privileged and wealthy, had a beautiful, immaculate home, a wonderful family network, so we did not feel the hardships as much as many ordinary Iranians.

'But in Betty's book, I became the symbol of all that was wrong with Iran. The book made it clear that no matter where we went, what we did or how long we were in America, deep down all Iranians are crazed, war-mongering religious zealots that want to destroy America at the first opportunity. Personally, from the way the book is written, it feels as if the authors believed that I had a switch in my brain, as if there's something in the Iranian air that caused me to turn into a monster as soon as I landed in Iran.'

'I'm not sure I understand why Betty decided she had to write a book,' someone asked. 'Was it for money?'

'I think the success of the book surprised even Betty. I think there's much more to it than that. All through the book Betty pits herself and Mahtob against me – it's a plea for custody. And who could fail to be moved and to do something to protect Mahtob by this description?

"Mahtob took in the words carefully, and as I saw her tearful young eyes trying to comprehend a new chill ran up my screaming spine, caused by a fresh, horrible thought. What if Moody really did kill me? What would become of Mahtob then? Would he kill her too? Or was she young and pliant enough that she would grow to accept this madness as the norm? Would she become a woman like Nasserine, or Essey, cloaking her beauty, her spirit, her soul, in the chador Would Moody marry her off to a cousin who would beat her and impregnate her with vacant-eyed, deformed babies?"

'When Betty relates an account of Mahtob cutting her arm and having it stitched without anesthetic. I should point out here that I have no recollection at all of such an incident. Anyway, during this scene I hold Mahtob firmly down, while the doctor stitches her wound– it is Betty that sheds a tear and not I. Another nail in my coffin. She also refers to the 'shadow of madness that descends upon' me."

'Indeed, the 'violence' soon escalates:

"Mahtob can come with me," Moody said. "I'll carry her."

"No," she screamed. He reached for her hand but she shied away...

Angered by her defiance, Moody grabbed her hand and jerked her away from me roughly. At the same time, he kicked her sharply in the back.

"No!" I yelled at him. Encumbered by the heavy chador I lunged after my daughter.

Moody immediately turned his wrath upon me, screaming at the top of his lungs, spitting out every English obscenity he could recall. I began to cry, suddenly impotent against his rage.

Now Mahtob tried to rescue me, pushing in between us. Moody glanced down at her as if she were an afterthought. In blind anger he backhanded her sharply across the face. Blood spurted from a cut on her upper right lip, spattering into the dust...

...Mahtob whimpered. Moody, unapologetic, sulked... I had to get my daughter and myself out of this nightmare before he killed us both.'

'In the book, Mahtob turns against me very quickly; just a few weeks after we arrived in Iran according to Betty, *'Mahtob could not conceal her revulsion for him.'*

'All of the interactions between Betty and Mahtob are based on wrong-doings performed by me and my family, and the intimate conspiracy between Betty and Mahtob that develops as a result.

'The authors use Mahtob as a tool to help demonise my family - and we are clearly held up as a "fair representation" of all Iranians. In essence, the book turns both Iran and I into a terrifying, irrational and incomprehensible monster. Of course the interaction between two human beings is complex, much more complex than this – as it is between two countries.

'Unless I'm very much mistaken, Betty was already taken care of financially before she even wrote the book. We had several hundred thousand dollars in property and savings, and we left all of it in America, earning interest, ready for our return.

'Our subsequent divorce and child custody hearing was a travesty. Within weeks Betty had claimed all our US assets, divorced me, won sole custody of Mahtob and filed a restraining order against me. I received notice of my court date in February 1992, via a letter sent to my sister eight months after the hearing had taken place.

The US judge who held the hearing, Patrick Reed Joslyn has since said that this was a mistake and that I would receive the 'red carpet treatment' should I wish to contest the decision in his courtroom. "No one represented Mr Mahmoody, no one filed; he was served from ordinary mail," he said when he was asked about the case by a journalist in 2004. "The summons was mailed in April 1991, *after* the hearings. This was a *fait accompli*. Should Mr Mahmoody wish it, he would have no trouble re-visiting the case in my court."

Of course, I could not get into America to test the judge's promise. Even if did have the opportunity to revisit his courtroom I suspected that I wouldn't get fair treatment as the same judge, speaking to the same journalist, said: "Remember the ones who took control of the Embassy, abused American citizens? If I were in charge there'd be a lot of dead Iranians. Seems to be the only way you can deal with these irrational folks. They don't believe in the law." He hardly sounds impartial to me!

'In the book Betty said I had run up credit card debts of $4,000 "buying lavish gifts" for my relatives and were in arrears to the Internal Revenue Service. I do not think so. At least Betty admitted that we *"we had a house full of expensive furniture and two cars. We also owned a rental home in Corpus Christi,"* and that we *"still had assets, accumulated during the lucrative years of Moody's practice."*

'She used her book to create a different world, a world where I absorbed her worst aspects and experiences and then magnified them for the reader.'

'For example: *"It was also fixed firmly in my mind that I could never, ever trust in the health of Moody's shattered mind."*

'I was also *"driven by a madness that allowed him no peace."*

'She even turned my own family against me, recreating her own isolation on confusion in Iran and conflicts with her own family in America. She stripped me of my medical qualifications, saying that I never earned a license to practice in Iran.'

I stopped speaking. I'd lost track of time. The energy that had until then enthused me suddenly left and I looked down sadly. Quietly, I said: 'In this book, all that was left of me was a monster, a growling beast of the lowest order.'

'This book and its politics tore apart my beautiful country where I had grown up in the midst of a loving extended family, where my ancestors had lived for 3,000 years and which had given the world peaches, the game of chess and the word for "paradise". Thanks to this book, my country - which also gave the world its first declaration of human rights - was reduced to a few unrepresentative, unpleasant stereotypical and racist images.

'It broke my heart.'

I looked up.

The Man from the Ministry was smiling.

I started to gather my things in readiness to end the lecture - but it wasn't quite over yet.

'Dr Mahmoody, can I ask you a question?

I stopped and smiled. An earnest-looking young man was standing up

'Sure,' I said.

I was tired however, and wanted to get out into the fresh air, to walk then sit on a bench somewhere and collect my thoughts.

'Forgive me but there's something I'd really like to know.'

'Please, go ahead.'

'What is the first thing you'd say to Mahtob if she walked into this room right now?'

I froze; the silence was total. When I spoke, I answered as if Mahtob had indeed just walked in.

'I am so sorry. So sorry that I was not a strong enough or wise enough man to keep us together as a family. I am so sorry that you have had to suffer for my sins. You probably hate me now, but perhaps, just perhaps, there are some happy memories of me waiting to be stirred.

'Remember when we were in Tehran and it snowed? Our yard was knee-deep and we ran outside to make a snowman. You used a carrot for the nose, walnuts for his eyes. And then you took your own scarf, it was purple, and wrapped it around the snowman's neck. When I now close my eyes and think of that wonderful day I can see it perfectly. Do you remember your red bicycle? How my heart raced when I let you go for the first time and you pedalled away from me! I still have it. Sometimes, I take it out just to look at it and try to remember how happy we were. And the watch you picked out for me for my birthday...it still works perfectly.

"I remember that when you were little, I used to ask you: "How much do I love you?"

My voice cracked. I cleared my throat.

"You would throw your arms wide and say: 'This much, Daddy. This much-'"

I picked up my briefcase, hurried out and kept walking, letting my legs take me somewhere, anywhere.

CHAPTER TWENTY THREE
THE COUNTRY OF PARADOX

If you had told me in 1984 that I would still be in Iran in 2009, then I would have laughed at you. I suppose that twenty-five years later, I can no longer consider myself American, certainly that I am less American than when I arrived here a quarter of a century ago. At the same time, I do not consider myself fully Iranian and even today I often feel like a stranger in my own land. I am a paradox within a paradox.

After I returned to Tehran - the City of Contradiction in the Country of Paradox – ending my self-imposed exile in Arak, I watched with happiness as without war, the irrepressible people of Iran started to enjoy their lives again.

Over the past three decades Tehran has become a different city altogether. To start with, it has grown out of all proportion from four million in 1979 to fifteen million, about two thirds of whom are under thirty and have no memory of the revolution.

I also watched as Iran gradually become more liberal (by Iranian standards – and before taking a sudden step backwards in recent years) thanks mainly to reformist President Mohammad Khatami who, in 1997, was voted in on a promise of change by enthusiastic young first-time and female voters.

In Iran, there is no voter registration or roll. Iranians aged sixteen and over can vote in any polling station as long as they present their national identification book, or *Shenasnameh*, which is stamped with a unique print when they vote. The Iranian President is determined through an absolute majority, so whoever gets 50%+1 of the votes is the winner.

Unfortunately, although this system has been in place since the revolution, we do not live in a democracy. Although the majority of people in Iran make use of their vote, and overwhelmingly vote for the candidates that seem to them to be the most democratic, change is always blocked by the hardliners who keep hold of the real power through the judiciary and the Guardian Council, an unelected conservative supervisory body.

The Guardian Council have abolished the reformist press, vetoed Parliamentary election candidates, and are behind the arrest torture and assassination of many liberals and other activists. The unelected supreme leader and the conservative clerics and lawyers control the courts, the army, the media, and political councils and very nearly run the economy. The Guardian Council also get to veto who will run in parliamentary elections – so a democracy we are not.

However, the young, always a driving force in Iran, are still changing our country today – sometimes in unexpected ways, such as the modern phenomenon that is the blog. Our rulers are my age, the people who lived through the Islamic Revolution a quarter of a century ago are now a minority and are struggling to contend with the young, intelligent, vibrant, passionate and fearless young people of Iran.

Today in Iran, the blog is the equivalent of the Arabian walled garden where one says whatever one pleases. Thanks in part to our high literacy rate (90 per cent, even including rural areas) over 64,000 blogs are written in Farsi – that's more blogs than Spain, Germany, Italy, China and Russia.

Blogs tend to be a lot more political in Iran. Prominent writers and journalists are able to bypass state censorship. While many citizens simply record their daily experiences giving insightful snapshots of life in Iran, many student groups and NGOs use their blogs as meeting rooms, as a place where they can decide agendas, make speeches and plan their activities.

I think that so many Iranians write blogs because they consider it their right to be able to tell the world what life is really like in Iran. The Internet gives Iranians that rare and precious commodity: the right to express themselves publicly.

As I've mentioned before, any foreigner who visits Tehran is immediately struck by the gap between the reality of Iranian society and the image cultivated by the regime – this is clearly demonstrated by the blogs.

Unfortunately, there is a price to be paid. The Internet is a hazardous form of communication for Iranians. While we are used to the hardline judiciary shutting down newspapers, magazines and publishers, many bloggers have recently been arrested because they've posted something online that the leadership didn't like. This has done nothing to stem the tide, however.

Public expression is changing too. These days in Tehran, the same shopkeepers who refused to serve women who were not wearing a chador now have teenage daughters who barely cover their hair and dress to impress when out in public. That is not to say that the repression of women has ended – far from it.

The repression of Iranian women played a large role in Betty's book and while what most of what she said was wrong, I hope I have made it clear in this book that Iranian women have been forced to endure many unpleasant hardships since the revolution.

By 2001, women's rights were at the forefront of political campaigning. Fourteen women were in Parliament. Perhaps the most influential of these was the Islamic feminist Faezeh Rafsanjani, daughter of an ex-president. Not only a respected MP and academic, Rafsanjani also ran a magazine and proved her sporting prowess by riding horses for the Iranian Olympic team.

During this time the legal marital age was raised from nine to thirteen, single women were allowed to study abroad and custody provisions were improved for divorced mothers. I should point out that the average age for women who marry is twenty-three and this is yet another instance of the difference in attitude between the people and the ruling conservative clerics. The vast majority of Iranians are horrified at the idea of thirteen-year-olds getting married – as far as they are concerned, the law legitimises child abuse.

Of course, there was (and still is) a very long way to go and there is a huge wall we have yet to break through. On 2 August 2003 Parliament unanimously voted in favour of joining the UN Convention on the Elimination of all forms of Discrimination Against Women. The Guardian Council said it violated Iranian and Islamic Sharia law and so Iran didn't sign up.

The chador and to a lesser extent the hijab have remained firmly in place as dramatic visual symbols of female oppression in Western minds and the chador still today makes regular appearances on book covers – including some recent editions of *Not Without My Daughter*.

Today, the chador is still worn in poorer neighbourhoods and in almost all the provinces, even though it is really no longer mandatory. In recent years, especially in Tehran, chadors and hijabs have gradually started to fade from the streets. Young women have cast them aside in favour of less modest, close fitting brightly-coloured coats and headscarves that barely conceal trendy hairstyles.

These days, the *Komiteh* and the newly formed 'Special Units' (teams of moral police wearing black berets and driving black cars) seem to arbitrarily choose what's right and wrong in terms of dress. Usually, they enforce a clampdown in spring, when the weather starts to get warmer and women are instructed to dress more modestly. Often, the clampdowns seem half-hearted and within a few weeks, everything is back the way it was. The choice now rests with the woman and her family. In Tehran, the chador had already by this time largely been replaced by the manteau, a shapeless overcoat (which Betty spells 'mantoe' throughout her book). Figure-hugging hip-length coats topped off with a light, almost see-through cloth that barely covers a fashionable and expensive haircut, have now replaced manteau in Tehran.

Most women in Iran will tell you that the chador and the hijab is the least of their worries; what is more important is to change the institutional discrimination inherent in Iranian society and the laws that interfere with women's rights.

A wife can only ask for a divorce if she can prove that her husband is either impotent, a drug user, unable to provide financially or has been absent from the home for six months. A mother has the rights to custody of a child only up to the age of seven; or girls aged thirteen and over and boys over the age of fifteen can decide who they want to stay with.

Having said that, the legally binding marriage contract is drawn up by the registrars prior to the ceremony and it is quite possible for the engaged couple to agree upon equal rights in case of divorce, to agree to joint child custody rights and so on. Such agreements – as the one Betty and I put our names to - remain popular and many registry offices have ready printed copies of them.

Again true to Iranian contradiction, although women are repressed publicly, any visit to an Iranian home - the most important institution in Iran - will leave you in no doubt as to who is really in charge of family life. Iranian women are powerful, determined and fearless as they continue to push forward against the established order. They are able to influence their menfolk and their children at home and this is where change amongst the youth of today is coming from.

Meanwhile, public campaigns have continued to gather strength. Shirin Ebadi, the Nobel-prize winner, author and human rights lawyer has recently won a lot of mainstream support. She has the right approach to change in Iran; all that's needed to improve human rights, Ebadi says, is a more intelligent interpretation of Islam. I agree, and I think Islam is compatible with democracy.

Iranians don't like being lectured by Americans about democracy, especially as the USA has set such a poor example. The Supreme Court's decision in 2000 to award the presidency to George Bush in the interests of the country, despite his second-place showing in the popular vote and a very questionable victory in the Electoral College, hardly seemed democratic.

Having said that, I, like many in Iran, believe that democracy is our best hope. Democracy in the West is shaped by Western culture and history and the same applies to Iran. Islam is the foundation of our culture and therefore it will have to influence our democracy. The problem is that Islam must adjust to democracy as well. Many influential politicians and clerics disagree, which is not surprising really, seeing as democracy threatens their divine right to rule.

Iran is still a land of contradictions and the root of this, I have come to realise, is the constant conflict between the will of the people and the will of our leaders. For example, despite the moral clampdowns, which have increased under President Mahmoud Ahmadinejad since he came to power in 2005 (he says he wants a return to the values of the revolution) the young still have no trouble in finding drink- and drug-fuelled[7] parties in Tehran where semi-naked women cavort amongst intoxicated teenage boys. The *Pasdaran* and the *Komiteh* are concerned with *public* morality and so almost never leave the streets, never daring to venture inside people's homes, nightclubs, cafes and so on.

Even our celebrities have surprised us with very public sex scandals, one of which came to light right in the midst of these clampdowns. Zahra

---

7   According to official figures, Tehran has two million drug users, and there has recently been a sharp rise in the number of drug addicts among women and young people – heroin in particular is on the increase.

Ebrahimi – arguably Iran's most famous actress - played the part of a well-behaved, devout young Muslim girl in the country's favourite soap opera. She seemed just as virtuous in real life - until that is one day in 2006 when a film that was never supposed to have seen the light of day appeared on the Internet– a home-made video of her and her then boy-friend having sex.

Soon, despite the *Komiteh*, it was being sold on every street corner. Her boyfriend left for foreign lands while Ebrahimi said it wasn't her in the video – but the millions of Iranians who carefully and repeatedly studied the film disagreed. As the investigation continued, the couple declared that they'd performed a temporary marriage (a convenient loophole which enables unmarried couples to try all the delights of marriage before they opt for the permanent version). The video sold by the tens-of-thousands, making some people very wealthy. This inspired a flood of copycat videos made by lewd young couples hoping to get rich.

It seems incredible that at the same time as such scandals and videos are making headlines and selling like hot cakes, Iranian women are still being given a hundred lashes or even being stoned to death for crimes such as adultery in some parts of Iran. All it takes is four male witnesses to condemn a woman.

Even in Tehran, executions still play a part in everyday life. In 2007, after a harsh crackdown on criminal gangs, I passed by a scaffold on top of a large flat bed truck on a busy street. I stopped in horror when I saw a noose dangling from the arm of a crane. Our president wanted to make a very public example of some of the condemned but I walked quickly away and nobody turned out to watch. Plans for other public executions were shelved but over three hundred people were still executed that year.

These clampdowns usually work as distractions for the rebellious among us, as they usually come at times when the government is about to imple-ment an unpleasant new decision or law – such as the decision to ration petrol to prepare for increasingly likely UN or US and European imposed sanctions. We need to import petrol thanks to our inadequate oil refining abilities (appropriately enough, this is blamed on US sanctions). Nobody wants to protest about such unpopular measures during a clampdown, lest they end up in "Hotel Evin".

But true to its contradiction, although Iran still executes many prisoners, Evin prison has changed dramatically in recent years. In an effort to improve its image abroad (motivated largely by the international press as well as a few brave Iranian campaigners) the running of the prison has improved enormously. The government is always quick to offer foreign reporters a tour of the facility and has transformed the running and design of the prison and delights in pointing out (especially in the wake of the Abu Ghraib scandal, CIA rendition and abuses at the Guantánamo detention facility) how Iran compares favourably to the West in the treatment of its political prisoners. Even Iranian-American political prisoners have been allowed to travel back to the States where they speak of the "ordinariness" of the prison. This is not to say that once the reporters have left and the steel doors have clanged shut behind them that abuses never take place. Reports have emerged that drug use is rife inside Iran's prisons and little is done about this as prisoners' dependency on these drugs makes them easier to handle.

President Ahmadinejad wanted to make sure that the British sailors who were arrested for straying into Persian waters in 2007 were extended the finest Iranian hospitality before their release. Part of this involved presenting the sailors with brand new but ill-fitting suits to wear in front of the TV cameras. The Western media seized upon the fact that they were poorly-cut, stating that they had been dressed by the same tailor who cuts the cheap suits favoured by President Ahmadinejad. In fact, a much superior tailor than the one the president favoured had provided the suits, but the West understandably missed the point.

Sadly, like most Iranians who have never left the country, President Ahmadinejad is unaware that tarof and other Iranian social customs are alien concepts in the West. The President has also misjudged his own people's willingness to stand idly by as he seeks tighter controls over the country and constant re-election. I watched from my apartment during the summer of 2009 as a million people took to the streets of Tehran once more, thirty years after the revolution, to protest the fixing of the election - carried out by all the president's men.

It was strange to see the people marching past Gucci and Versace billboards, through the renamed Victory Square, Revolution Square and Freedom

Square before they fled home again, pursued by tear gas and bullets. Then came the ensuing arguments over the number of dead (somewhere between 36 and 72 in the initial June protests), which brought tears to my eyes. One of the deaths, that of 27-year-old Neda Agha-Soltan was broadcast around the world thanks to YouTube and Facebook and inspired a documentary film. The President can hide his wrongdoings no longer.

Although talk of revolution was in the air - the protesters called themselves the Green Revolution (after opposition candidate Mir-Hossein Mousavi's campaign colour) - the clamour eventually died away. The time wasn't right and the president wasn't going anywhere – although he had cheated, he still had plenty of supporters. As a taxi driver once told me, "We little people simply want to get on with our lives in peace and with full stomachs". Unfortunately, those in crazy people in charge all too often make us suffer for some ridiculous goal that has no bearing on ordinary people's day-to-day lives.

Yes, life is difficult for us ordinary folk - no matter which country we are in, whether in the USA, which is still fighting its endless War on Terror, or in Iran, which is still struggling to give our thirty-year-old Revolution some kind of voice in the modern world.

Sometimes we make life difficult for ourselves. By coming to Iran, I had hoped to give Betty and I a new start in life. But of course we remain the same people wherever we are.

It was, in fact, the beginning of the end.

CHAPTER TWENTY FOUR
THE LAST RESORT

At the end of her book, Betty wrote:

Mahtob and I now live with the reality that we may never be free from Moody's ability to lash out at us from nearly half a world away. His vengeance could fall upon us at any time, in person, or through the vehicle of one of his innumerable legion of nephews. Moody knows that if he could somehow spirit Mahtob back to Iran, the laws of his alien society would support him completely.

What Moody may not realize is that my vengeance is as total as his. I now have powerful friends in the United States and in Iran who would never allow him to triumph. I cannot detail the extent of my precautions; suffice it to say that Mahtob and I are now living under assumed names in an undisclosed location-somewhere in America.

Well, just as Betty stated, her 'vengeance' had indeed been 'total'. It seemed to me that there was little chance that any of my daughter's happy memories of our life together would survive.

But I will never give up. I am not a quitter. I see fathers with children every day and every day I think of Mahtob. I want to meet my daughter. I want her to know who I am. Although I am forever grateful for the precious six years I was able to share with my baby, my loss of Mahtob has become the defining moment of my life, something that has tortured me ever since.

So many of my everyday memories of those first six years have been lost. I tell other parents that every single second with your child is precious and that every event and memory should be cherished. As I wrote this book I thought about all the little things Mahtob and I would do, like reading stories, going for walks, rowing on our little boat, playing in the garden and collecting the prettiest leaves. These 'everyday' memories are there but faint, mere impressions now - like old videotape that has been replayed a thousand times, the footage is scratched and faded.

If I think of these scenes too hard and look for details, like what we talked about, whether we were cold in the boat, what we did with the leaves we collected and what stories I told, or what Mahtob was wearing, for example, then they flit away into greyness. If I relax I can see them return and start to spool through my mind's cinema projector, faded but just about there.

I wish that in her book, Betty had set down some of these scenes like these while her memories were still fresh, so I would have more reminders about times when the three of us shared wonderful moments together, as I know we did. I hold onto those memories that are still sharp for dear life – the day of Mahtob's birth, her first birthday, riding her bike for the first time...

The day she gave me a watch and told me she loved me so much...

Some 'friends' told me to forget about Mahtob, that it had been so long that I should get used to the idea that she's gone and that I will never see her again and that I should not disturb her by trying to get in touch.

'Imagine it's your child,' I tell them, 'would you forget them?'

I am certain that the overwhelming majority of parents would find it impossible to give up on finding their children, no matter what the circumstances or how many years had passed. Overwhelmingly, estranged parents want their children to know the truth about them, or at least a chance to state their case.

I never remarried. I have no other children. To me the idea of marrying again remained impossible. As far as I am concerned I am still married to Betty, just as I am Mahtob's father and I won't betray my family. To give my life purpose in the meantime, I have buried myself deep in my work and it is this, alongside the hope that comes from my innate Iranian sense of rights, the loss of my right to see and be with my daughter, that keeps me going. I remain hopeful that one day I will see Mahtob again - but I know it will take a miracle.

Every day I pray for that miracle.

Today, Mahtob is living in the USA and, to my delight I hear that she has, in a sense followed in the footsteps of my mother and father as well as myself, and is now a medical practitioner. I have tried writing to her via the

American Medical Association but I don't know if my mail ever arrived and I wouldn't be surprised if Mahtob didn't read it if it did. I know Mahtob wants nothing to do with me but I always hope that one day she might change her mind.

To this end, the only remaining chance I had of getting my daughter to hear my side of the story was to try and publish it. This book grew from the notes I used for my lectures given to the politics and history students at Tehran University, something I have found to be a continually fascinating, if daunting challenge. I still find myself fighting for composure as I struggle with painful, yet treasured memories.

When a few years ago, a student first put the idea to me: 'Dr Mahmoody, why don't you write a book?' my first thought was that nobody wanted to read my story.

'Why should anyone believe me?' I asked the student, and the class. 'What would be my motivation?'

'Well, you have no need for money, so they cannot say you are in it for financial reasons.'

'This would be a courageous act,' said another. 'Betty describes you as a coward but this would be a brave thing to do. You would, by reawakening interest in the story and by disagreeing strongly with Betty's account, open yourself up to criticism from around the world. Surely that is not the behaviour of a cowardly abuser.'

Seeing the blogs and some of the responses to them opened my eyes to the possibility that enough people in the world today might be interested in my side of the story to make it publishable. I could have tried a blog but I couldn't risk raising the ire of the regime. I also didn't want to involve my family in my present day activities in case I got into trouble, so I opted for the temporary privacy of authorship.

I thought long and hard about the effect this book might have on Mahtob but I remain confident that, as she is now thirty-years-old and working in the US under a different name, she is mature enough and able enough to cope with hearing my side of the story.

As time went on, I started to think that perhaps my book could be a bit more than just my version of events. I thought that perhaps readers would like to know a bit more about my life in Tehran, our customs and ways and so I have done my best to describe such things in an effort to create a bit understanding between East and West.

God knows, we need it.

In March 2009, Hollywood attempted to reach out to Iran when an ambassadorial delegation travelled from the USA to Tehran. It was a group full of big-hitters and included *American Beauty* star Annette Bening, and *Field of Dreams* director Phil Robinson. It also included Sid Ganis, president of the Academy of Motion Picture Arts and Sciences, William Horberg, producer of *The Kite Runner*, and Alfre Woodard, who acted in *Desperate Housewives*. They had travelled to Iran as part of a charm offensive billed as a "creative exchange" with Iranian filmmakers.

The delegation had been invited to Iran by Khane Cinema (Cinema House), our country's biggest film group, which is of course subject to the authority of the Ministry of Culture and Islamic Guidance. It was scheduled to hold training workshops on acting, directing, documentary-making and other aspects of the business.

The other key part of this trip was aimed at bridging a gulf of mutual misunderstanding.

We should have embraced them – but sadly, we didn't.

Mistrust of Hollywood had already prompted President Mahmoud Ahmadinejad to turn down a request made by Oliver Stone, the director of *JFK*, to film a documentary about him. Stone had made controversial documentaries about Fidel Castro and Yasser Arafat, so the request wasn't quite as crazy as it sounded. But, in my opinion, in this case the president was quite right to refuse. No newspaper report mentioned the fact that Oliver Stone was the scriptwriter of *Midnight Express* – for which he won an Oscar and which he kept despite later being forced to apologise by the Turkish government as well as many American campaigners for his overblown fictional adaptation of the book which featured simplistic and inaccurate racial stereotyping of the Turkish people.

President Ahmadinejad tore into the delegation after they arrived – or more precisely, this was left to the his arts adviser, Javad Shamghadri who requested that the delegation apologise for Hollywood's past sins against Iran before they were introduced to leading figures in Iran's film industry.

"[Iranian] cinema officials will only have the right to have official sessions with ... Hollywood moviemakers when they apologise to the Iranians for their thirty years of insults and slanders," Shamghadri told the news agency ISNA. "The Iranian people and our revolution have been repeatedly unjustly attacked by Hollywood. We will believe Obama's policy of change when we see change in Hollywood too, and if Hollywood wants to correct its behaviour towards Iranian people and Islamic culture then they have to officially apologise."

It was a shame because ordinary Iranians, who – as I've already mentioned, - eagerly watch Hollywood productions on pirated DVDs and on illegal satellite channels would have loved to have seen a little real life Hollywood action in Iran.

And what were Hollywood's sins? Well, the blockbuster *300* for a start. Produced by Warner Brothers, it told the story of a battle between Greeks and Persians at Thermopylae in 480BC. Shamghadri described *300* as "psychological warfare" and had already complained to the UN that it subjected Iranians to racial stereotyping.

Then there was *Alexander*, a 2004 biopic about Alexander the Great, directed by Oliver Stone, criticised for its sympathetic portrayal of the ancient Macedonian king, whom Iranians blame for the destruction of Persepolis in 330BC.

Also under fire was the 2008 film *Body of Lies,* starring Leonardo di Caprio and Russell Crowe and directed by Ridley Scott. The film was picked out because the director had chosen to show the hair of the Iranian female character, played by actress Golshifteh Farahani as she 'gets together' shall we say, with Mr di Caprio's American character.

These all seemed like fairly ridiculous criticisms to most Iranians but I thought, perhaps, that the Ministry actually had a fair point when it came to *The Wrestler*. Its main character, played by Mickey Rourke, smashed a pole carrying Iran's national flag across his knee. It also featured a bad-guy wrestler called the Ayatollah who wore a skimpy leotard in our country's colours.

I couldn't believe it when I saw that the last film on the list was *Not Without My Daughter*! Amazing! Even, after almost twenty years, that awful film was still getting under the government's skin!

The point is, I suppose, that in film and literature, not much has changed in the representation of Iran from *Not Without My Daughter* to the *Wrestler*.

As far as the West is concerned, thirty years after the Revolution we're still a country of bad guys. Ask anyone in the West abut Iran and they'll think of a crazy president trying to get hold of nuclear weapons – a regular James Bond villain.

Even one of the world's greatest storytellers – Steven Spielberg – cannot cope with an Iranian character in a lead role in one of his films. *The Terminal* was based in the true story of Mehran Nasseri, an Iranian exile who ended up stranded in Paris airport for fifteen years and wrote a book about his experience. In the film, the Iranian exile, played by Tom Hanks, is transformed into an Eastern European man by the name of Viktor. As one blogger pointed out, if Spielberg, who made the world fall in love with the ugly alien ET can't do the same for an Iranian, then what hope do we have?

Yes, it's a funny world. If, ten years ago, someone had said that one day the USA would want to build a missile defence system in Europe to protect the West from a potential missile attack (possibly nuclear) from Iran (and that these missiles were made in Iran), then I would have laughed heartily at the joke.

Although many Iranians are proud that we've been elevated to semi-superpower, many more find it quite amusing that Iran is at the centre of the United States', if not the worlds', attention today, partly because of its nuclear program (I can remember the international community stating that Iran was five years from obtaining 'the bomb' back in 1977. Apparently, we're still five years away) and partly because it's on the list with the comic Thunderbirds-like title: The Axis of Evil.

I, like most of my countrymen believe that all this attention comes from our ability to affect American lives through our vast oil reserves and our influence in Iraq and Afghanistan and that – thanks to the Revolution – we can't be influenced politically by the United States, so there's no other option for them but to take a confrontational stance and get the rest of the world to gang up on us as well.

And *Not Without My Daughter* had a role to play in creating that situation. And here I am, still trying - almost twenty years since the film, to tell my side of the story.

I feel like there's two of me out there. At the moment Betty landed in America after her 'escape' from Iran, a new, evil image of me, intoxicated by its birth, separated itself from me and walked off in the opposite direction in search of its own destiny. It has done rather better in attracting attention than I have. I want to, need to erase this other me, even after all this time. Mahtob is my only motivation. As I have already mentioned, I have no need for money, no political agenda (for an Iranian writing a book to be published in the West, I have been very critical of Iran), no desire for 'revenge' or 'justice'. I've nothing to lose but my freedom but, as the last grains pass through the hourglass, I've not got much of that left.

My first reaction once I'd realised that I'd probably lost Mahtob forever was to end the story there by killing myself. But that second catastrophic event, the Scud missile, made me realise that taking my own life was a useless and selfish act and that, as a doctor, I could still be of use.

Since that day I've always hoped I would see Mahtob again, but now, as I head towards life's exit door, I do realise that this is very unlikely. So I have to do something. I cannot die knowing that I did not try everything possible to reach my daughter. A book may yet reach her after I'm gone.

Until recently I did not think that anyone in the West would be interested in my side of the story. As I mentioned earlier, the Internet helped change all that and I have since learnt that there is enormous curiosity about what I have to say.

So this is my last shot at getting in touch with Mahtob. I've tried everything else. One of the many great ironies of my life story is that although Betty accused me of imprisoning her and Mahtob in Iran, it was Betty who ended up imprisoning me in my home country. I tried again and again, but my repeated requests for a passport were always rejected. This is the case with many Iranians (I was on quite a prestigious list as even one or two former presidents were also forbidden from leaving the country).

I couldn't believe it when, in 2005, they suddenly decided to give me a passport. But when I checked with the US Consul, they warned me that if I travelled to the US without a green card, I would be arrested and as for a green card, well I could forget that. Although I already knew this would be the case, I couldn't help myself and wept down the phone, begging them for help.

This moment was caught on film by a Finnish documentary team who made a short film about my side of the story. I travelled with them to Helsinki where I tried to contact Mahtob through her university, suggesting we meet in Finland, a neutral country. I would have preferred London perhaps – an easier and more familiar place for Mahtob to fly to but as the documentary makers were from Finland, then Helsinki made more sense. Besides, Iranian immigration asked fewer questions about Finland than England (regarded by the government as an enemy state). I was extremely nervous that Iranian Customs would stop me from travelling at the last minute.

As I passed through Mehrabad airport, I was interested to see that there were no anti-American posters this time. They'd been replaced with a much more neutral: 'Have a nice trip'.

Well, my trip was anything but nice. It was all in vain. There was, as I should have expected, no response and I simply left long messages on Betty and Mahtob's voicemails after the documentary makers travelled to America and managed to get hold of their phone numbers.

Not long after this, my health started to fail; soon I needed daily dialysis. Suddenly, after more than twenty years of waiting for my passport, I was no longer well enough to travel beyond Iran's borders.

So, maybe a book will work where all else has failed. I hope there will come a time when Mahtob picks up this book, reads the first page... and keeps going. Mahtob is in my thoughts every day. I love her as any father would love their daughter and I can only hope that her anger will fade, and she will forgive me.

In this account I have not exaggerated, nor have I tried to conceal anything. I took a breath, opened my heart and let go... I have simply told my story how it was - which has not been easy.

I made plenty of mistakes, I wasn't the best husband, I wasn't sensitive to Betty's needs, and so in a sense this book is both confession and apology.

In *Not Without My Daughter* (both the book and the film), I was transformed from a gentle husband and loving father into a violent tyrant practically overnight. To assume that moving to Iran brought out a monster that had always been lurking within me, dormant for the twenty years I lived in the USA and for the seven years Betty and I were married, was entirely incorrect.

In 1992, Betty wrote a second book *For the Love a Child*. It told the story of how *Not Without My Daughter* came about and the public reaction that followed. She also claimed that I came to the US to kill her and kidnap Mahtob - something I would never, ever have dreamt of doing (even if I had could have left Iran, let alone travel to the USA).

In the conclusion Betty wrote "It is always the children who pay most dearly for their parents' sins". I can only agree - by doing what she thought was best, Betty deceived Mahtob – and I wasn't strong and aware enough to stop it from happening. I pray that it isn't too late, although I fear it is, for Mahtob to realise just how much I love and miss her.

Today, Iran and the USA remain as divided as Betty and I. Having said that, I realise now, in finishing this book that I am really able at last to forgive Betty for what she did to me. Even though I would never have chosen this fate, my life through my work has had some worth. My beautiful Mahtob is happy, healthy and successful and as a parent I can't wish for more. Betty, you have done a great job in raising our daughter without me and for that I thank you.

In *Not Without My Daughter*, Betty says, in regard to one of my relatives who had written some published works:

"Detailing the duties of a child toward the father, he related a story about a dying father who longed to see his son one last time. Tears rolled down my cheeks. The words on the page in front of me blurred. My own father was dying, and I should be at his side."

I perhaps do not need to tell you how that statement has stuck with me since I read it. Just to see Mahtob one more time, to talk with her for a few moments is all I dream of.

Of course, I realise that this is highly unlikely. Thanks to the Internet I have been able to find some recent interviews with Mahtob and Betty. Although parts of these interviews make me feel particularly proud of Mahtob and happy for her in that they clearly demonstrate she is making the most out of life, they make difficult reading for me.

Mahtob has been quoted as saying that she is still afraid of me and does not want to have any contact. In one article she said: *"I feel like the father I loved so much died. I have already grieved that loss."*

In another newspaper I read: *"Mahtob is a great believer in collecting happiness. Every day she writes down five things that make her happy. She said people should have realistic expectations. She said, 'I will not ever have a normal life. You should write your own script for your life. God is out there and he has a master plan.'"*

Another statement has stayed with me even more. Betty finished her book with this about Mahtob, and this paragraph has long tortured me. Whenever I read it, it is as if a large, invisible hand is squeezing my heart:

"The readjustment to life in America has been difficult for Mahtob but she has responded with the resiliency of youth. She brings straight A's home from school, and she is once more a happy child radiating sunshine. At times she misses her daddy not the madman who held us hostage in Iran, but the loving father who once cherished us both."

Dearest Mahtob, I have always cherished you. I always will.

POSTSCRIPT

On August 23, 2009, almost twenty-five years to the day he arrived with Betty and Mahtob in Iran, Sayed Bozorg Mahmoody died in Tehran, aged seventy. The state news agency quoted his nephew, Majid Ghodsi, as reporting that he died in a hospital from kidney problems and other complications. Ghodsi said: "He thought of his daughter until the end."

Six weeks later, this article appeared in *The Orange County Register*, dated November 4, 2009:

You could have heard a pin drop as Not Without My Daughter *best-selling author Betty Mahmoody spoke about escaping an abusive relationship and fleeing 500 miles to a foreign country with her daughter Mahtob. Mahmoody and her daughter were the featured speakers at Human Options' sold-out contingent of 500 guests at its annual fall fundraising luncheon on October 28 at the Balboa Bay Club & Resort in Newport Beach. The luncheon's theme, "A Mother's Courage – Making a Journey from Fear to Victory," came alive with the mother/daughter story.*

The Mahmoody's plight, featured in the 1991 motion picture, "Not Without My Daughter," starring Sally Field, tells of Betty's husband's insistence on taking a two-week trip to Iran to visit his family in 1984 in the middle of the Iran/Iraqi war and at the end of the two weeks, refusing to let them go home to Michigan. Virtual prisoners in the family home for 18 months, while beating Betty and separating her from her daughter, the two finally escaped Tehran with the help of total strangers and crossed the snow-covered mountains that border Iran and Turkey on horseback. When it was too steep for the horses, they walked and actually had to be dragged the final yards to their freedom, "Do I believe in miracles?" Betty said. "Only by the grace of God did we make it home."

Mahtob continued the story, saying, "I was an angry six-year-old girl when we returned." They knew that Mahtob's father would not give up trying to get her back, so they changed their names and Betty got a permit for a concealed weapon while Mahtob wore a panic button 24/7. With the passage of time, however, Mahtob said she has learned three important lessons. "Learning to celebrate the good and the bad," she said, "we remembered the good times, growing up with mother making Persian food and celebrating my Persian heritage." Having an attitude of gratitude and the importance of focusing on service to others were her final lessons.

Along those lines, Betty is president and co-founder of One World: For Children, an organization designed to promote understanding between cultures and to offer security and protection to children of bi-cultural marriages.

Made in the USA
Middletown, DE
04 July 2019